I0055529

High-Performance Practice

Management, Marketing and Leadership

Results Press
Unit 229
#180, 8601 Lincoln Blvd.
Los Angeles, California
90045

www.theresultspress.com

ISBN-13: 978-0-9988905-4-8

First Edition

Dedication

I have been one of those fortunate few who has been staunchly supported by my pillars of family, friends and mentors. This book is for you.

To my Wife: I would not be a fraction of the man I am today without your love, support and intelligence.

To my children: I love you more than you will ever know, and without you this book would have been completed one year earlier ☺

High-Performance Practice

Management, Marketing and Leadership

Justin Bhullar, DMD

Results Press

CONTENTS

Chapter One: Controversy, Practicality and Experience 17

Chapter Two: Why 41

Chapter Three: You Can't Manage What You Can't Measure 57

Chapter Four: ROI-Based Marketing 93

Chapter Five: Relationships, Relationships, Relationships . 131

Chapter Six: Be a Leader, Not a Boss 167

Chapter Seven: McDonald's x Google = High-Performance Practice 211

Chapter Eight: Build Your Dream Team 249

Chapter Nine: Deeper Dive: Systems & Processes which will Help You Earn AND Retain More $$ 261

Chapter Ten: Be the Dumbest Person in the Room 287

A Moment of Humility and Vulnerability

I am the eldest of three children. My father's parents immigrated from India when he was only five years old. From a young age, my father inherited responsibilities no child should have to carry on his or her shoulders. The eldest of seven children, he sacrificed his entire childhood and best years to ensure his siblings and then eventually his children would have their basic needs met. My mother also immigrated from India in her late teens. She was the second youngest of nine children. I can only imagine what it must have been like for her to leave everything she'd ever known, including both of her parents, behind. Like many immigrants, they relocated in search for a better life. If they hadn't made these moves, I would not be where I am today.

My parents operated with integrity and worked so hard to make ends meet. Money was a major problem in my family. Negativity and chaos prevailed in my principle environment as I witnessed my parents working so hard yet making little progress.

My father believed the antidote to this struggle was more work. He would work harder and longer hours. He believed financial security came through a consistent income, which meant get a job and earn a paycheck. He would say, "Be anything you want to be, and I'll be happy, as long as you are independent and can support yourself."

On the other hand, my mother believed higher education was the solution. She also dreamed big and wanted for more. She would say, *"Become a doctor or dentist or some kind of professional."* Any actions on my part that suggested deviation from these expectations were met with a massive serving of guilt.

Guilt was a great motivator for me, especially knowing how hard my parents worked. I couldn't let them down. Guilt kept me going during the hard times. Needless to say, in high school, I set my sights on going to University and making my parents proud. However, the need for validation and approval would only take me so far.

Many of you likely excelled academically and have failed very little over the years. The same is not true for me. I struggled to receive good grades, read slower than the average person and battled with concentration. This made learning in a traditional academic setting difficult. My confidence suffered and I often felt anxious, alone and misunderstood. It wasn't a lack of intelligence, but rather an incorrect learning style and format for me. Unfortunately, audio books were not around back then. I felt like I was working 10 times as hard as everyone else to get the same results. I remember at one point I was told by my high school teacher that I would never become a dentist or a doctor. She said,

"You might be doing well here, but University is much more difficult. You should consider doing something else, because chances are you won't become a dentist or a doctor. Those are very competitive fields."

She wouldn't be the only person to tell me what I shouldn't or couldn't do. Each of these encounters discouraged me. I questioned whether I had what it took to achieve my goals. In addition to discouragement I felt anger. Who were they to tell me what I could and could not do? How could they know what my capabilities were? Anger was my second greatest motivator to encourage me to prove them wrong while proving to myself I could do it. I worked hard and got a scholarship to the University of British Columbia, only to lose it in the first year because I didn't maintain the minimum GPA. Let's just say I prioritized fun over progress and results during this period of time.

My journey into dental school was very unconventional. I was dealing with the discomfort of my parents' recent separation and struggling with my identity. I wasn't working hard, and I knew if I didn't do anything about it, I would not amount to anything. I completed six years of undergraduate studies on and off but never received a degree. I only had two good years out of six and the rest were not so good.

I worked so hard over those two years. I was all in.

Only two schools would take me without a degree and with two good years of grades. I applied to one of them, was waitlisted and eventually accepted. When I started dental school, I found it rigid and cookie-cutter. Up until that point in my life, I had never studied as hard as I did then. I felt like I was being taught a ton of useless, unnecessary information I wouldn't need to succeed as a dentist. I love to ask questions and am ultra-curious, a few of my professors did not enjoy my presence and outside of the box thinking.

Some of them made significant efforts to have me removed--a typical fear-based reaction when someone challenges your deep-seated belief system. Obviously, their plan didn't work, because I have written this book and am sharing my experiences with you about building multiple high-performance practices.

Obtaining my dental degree was one of the hardest things I had ever done. It made me feel as if I could do anything now. After all, I'd completed a degree that placed me in the top 3% of the world with respect to education. I felt significant, thought I had all of the answers and walked around with an inflated head. Then I bought my first practice and lost big time! I bought my second and then third and found myself stressed, overweight and underpaid. My relationships were suffering, and I was missing out on my family time.

In spite of these unfortunate early experiences, I have managed to grow, progress and achieve great success in

my practice acquisition and start-up journey. I was able to do this not because of luck, but rather a few things I believe are the true reasons for my success:
~I don't give up when I fail. I stand up, dust myself off and keep going.
~I am not afraid to ask for help and receive feedback
~I am creative and a great problem solver
~I surround myself by people whose strengths are my weaknesses
~I learned communication and sales skills.
~I welcome mentors and invested over $1.5 million dollars into my personal and professional education.
~I have compassion for other people and a genuine desire to uplift and see others grow.

I don't claim to have all the answers. I am always learning, am open minded and am willing to do what it takes to take things to the next level. I share all of this with you because I never want anyone to think I am perfect or that all of my offices run without issues. This is simply not true. Just like you, I encounter the same challenges any business faces.

Fortunately, with the information in this book, I am able to ensure I encounter these problems less frequently, creating time for me to work ON my business vs. IN my business. In turn, working on my business has allowed me to succeed and help others succeed along the way. In my opinion, progress contributes greatly to happiness and fulfillment, so that's what I strive for in all areas of my life. My wish for you is that you will be able to create high-performance practices of your own.

Be Aware of Your Strengths and Weaknesses

Our gifts (aka: strengths) often times are the things we accomplish with little effort and yield great joy. Try this exercise: a) Make a list of tasks that you complete in your life and business that seem relatively effortless and are enjoyable b) Now do the opposite (hard/unenjoyable). This strategy will assist you in composing a list of your strengths and weaknesses. I encourage you to consider having an open discussion about this topic with your spouse, friends, and team members. The people closest to you may see something you don't. Lastly you can utilize a resource such as StrengthsFinder 2.0 by Gallup to supplement what you have already learned (do not rely on SF 2.0 alone)

Definition of a High-Performance Practice

A high-performance practice is a business which allows the leader or owner to do work, be with people and find a place that brings them joy. It is an environment with a fun and positive culture that is productive and profitable. A high-performance practice affords the owner the opportunity to provide for his or her team, family and community, leaving a positive impact on each. Furthermore, it provides the owner with both time and money!

Disclaimer: Sounds too good to be true? That's because it is. We are not aiming for 100% here. If we can get this right 80% of the time, then we are way ahead of our peers and colleagues.

If this is what you want, then read on. I can't tell you how excited I am to be able to share this with you.

***

In **Chapter One**, here we discuss some of the myths circulating in dentistry today, the Controversy, Practicality and Experience may disturb or intrigue you.

Chapter Two will explore the Why and will be a nice, light introduction into the impetus of building a high-performance practice. Although most would consider a soft topic like exploring purpose a little woohoo, you won't make that mistake. This chapter will really get you to start thinking critically about what you think you know about yourself.

Chapter Three is a tactical discussion called You Can't Manage What You Can't Measure. You will be challenged to create duplicable and scalable systems using objective measurements for accountability.

In **Chapter Four**, we get into detailed and heavy content. We will explore ROI-Based Marketing. You probably guessed it will be heavy on the strategy with a healthy dollop of metrics.

Chapter Five is focused on Relationships, Relationships, Relationships. You have read books and taken courses about relationships before, but not like this. I will position the topic within the context of a high-performance practice.

Chapter Six is midway. Be A Leader, Not a Boss. Most entrepreneurs and business owners have trouble making this distinction...until now.

Chapter Seven is McDonald's x Google = High Performance Practice, though it is definitely so much more than what you might imagine. The focus is on building a practice by design instead of by default. Systems are the key to achieving consistent and repeatable results. However, great service and ingenuity require great people. Your lethal weapon is relying on 'A' players. That means hiring the right people, training them, giving them authorship and empowering them to use their best judgment.

Chapter Eight is fun and entertaining but no less challenging as you work through how to Build Your Dream Team. Who should you look for and how you get them onto your team are just two of the topics to fill the gaps.

Chapter Nine starts the home stretch--Deeper Dive: Systems & Processes That Will Help You Earn AND Retain More $$. This is content-loaded and information-rich about client care as a business and how to build the foundation of your high-performance practice.

We take it home in **Chapter Ten**--Be the Dumbest Person in the Room. This is a nice cool down from the previous chapters and focus on how to be a better version of you. Here's a hint--you need the help of others.

Throughout this, book pay attention to areas where you stop reading, stop listening or get anxious or angry. By observing these reactions, you can learn much about deep-seated beliefs that are not serving you well.

When you disagree, is it because the content is false? Or is it because you've tried it and it didn't work? Is it because another course/mentor told you to do it another way, or perhaps it's that you're afraid to implement it and fail?

For me, it was always one or a combo of the above that resulted in these reactions. Take note of your responses and learn a little more about the internal empire you have spent years building. The perceptions and beliefs that no longer serve you are only holding you back. You may be stagnating, or even worse, regressing.

One of my favorite quotes by Alvin Toffler is, "The illiterate of the 21st century will not be those who cannot read and write. Rather those who cannot learn, unlearn, and relearn."

Throughout this book, you will have much unlearning to do before you can relearn. I know this because at each new venture, with each new turn in the road life brings for me, I find myself doing a lot of unlearning. All of this is necessary before I can process new information which will serve me well.

It is my sincere hope that this content serves you as well as it does me. It has allowed me to build multiple profitable practices that have allowed me the freedom to live life on my terms, provide for my family, positively impact others and support my community. For those of you who have no desire to have multiple businesses, it all starts with one and you can stop there if you wish. Whether you are building one or multiple high-performance practices, the principles here are the same. I want you to be able to live on your terms and create a lifestyle unique to you--a life that truly fulfills you.

CHAPTER ONE –

Controversy, Practicality and Experience

"Things are not always what they seem; the first appearance deceives many; the intelligence of a few perceives what has been carefully hidden."
~Phaedrus

We all go into dentistry wanting to help people, create a great lifestyle for ourselves (and with our family, if applicable) and have the freedom that comes with being the captain of our own ship. This is the dream. In pursuit of this dream, we sacrifice much of our twenties--delaying social interaction and missing opportunities for earning income and investing. We are subjected to the thoughts, behaviors and beliefs of our colleagues and educators, which may or may not serve us well. Some of these beliefs, behaviors and thoughts are new to us. Perhaps originally all you wanted to do was graduate and get a job, but now you have been sold the idea of opening your own practice and running a business.

Maybe you were open-minded and hoped to perform all facets of dentistry, but someone convinced you that you should stick with the basics and leave the implants, orthodontics and full-mouth rehabs to the specialists. Perhaps they sold you on the idea success in dentistry is based on doing great dentistry and nothing else.

"Do good work and the rest will take care of itself."

*"Invest in your dental education
and you will make more money than you can spend."*

They sold you the idea that in order to be successful in dentistry, you need to spend money to make money and buy a Cone Beam CT, laser and in-house scanning/milling unit. I don't know what you specifically have been sold, but it is likely some version of that. Do you know a so-called *successful* practice owner who drives the car you want, lives in the home you want and has the million-dollar practice of your dreams? I knew several when I first graduated, but as I dug deeper and began to embark on my own pursuit of this dream, I discovered the truth.

A Few Controversial Topics

- Only specialists should be doing orthodontics, cosmetic dentistry, oral surgery, periodontics and other advanced procedures.
- Dental practices only fail 1% of the time.
- The million-dollar practice owner you admire is healthy, wealthy and living the dream.

- Do good dentistry, invest in your dental CE and buy advanced technology so patients will beat a path to your door.
- Every dentist should own a practice and practice ownership is your ticket to freedom.
- If you need to market your practice, you're not a great dentist. (Believe it or not, I still hear this today.)
- Corporate dentistry is ruining your chances of becoming a profitable practice owner.
- Rapid debt reduction is not necessary.
- Practice ownership is the fastest path to paying off debt.

The list goes on, but for the purposes of this chapter, I'll cap it right there.

This is some of the false information I was sold, and I am here to explain you can have the career of your dreams if you think objectively, question and validate the advice you receive and begin to think logically vs. emotionally. For more experienced owners or clinicians, some of this may not apply, or may be a *tell me something I don't know* situation, but I believe there is something to be learned for everyone here.

I believe the majority of people have good intentions. Most set out to share information they trust will positively impact their friends, clients or colleagues. The issue is that it's difficult to measure intention. It is also difficult to sift through information when it is coming at us at high speed.

Lastly, many people speak with conviction about topics they know a lot about but have no personal experience to support it. Experience trumps knowledge. In other words, would you rather learn from the person who studies about other businesses and simply reports their findings? Or would you prefer to learn from the professional who studies business, owns a business and shares their observations through experiences? I am not a genius, but I would choose the second person.

Only specialists should be doing orthodontics, cosmetic dentistry, endodontics, oral surgery, periodontics and other advanced procedures

This statement is driven by a scarcity, fear and ego. The scarcity mindset that perpetuates this level of commentary is based on a fear that there is not enough dentistry to go around. I find the individuals spreading this misinformation are typically in practices that are underperforming. I have multiple friends who are dental specialists. Those who have an abundant mindset tend to uplift and encourage other docs to perform *specialty* procedures. In fact, they help to educate them. Those with a scarcity mindset tend to judge, discourage and throw other doctors under the bus when they make a mistake or experience failure. Interestingly enough, my specialist friends with the abundant mindset have thriving practices. Guess who their number one referral source is? It's the general dentist that does the “specialty procedures.”

The ego part is self-explanatory. It comes down to the level of thinking that no one can do it better than me. At the end of the day, this may be true, but how will you know unless you give others a chance to get the education, give them encouragement and allow them to execute. If you're reading this and thinking what a jerk this guy is belittling specialties or undermining their skill--not at all. Please don't take it that way. I routinely perform IV sedation, oral surgery and do basic implant procedures in my office. We encourage our doctors to seek out CE in any area in which they are interested in expanding their skill sets. As a result, we perform 90% of specialty procedures in-house. We still have great relationships with our specialists to whom we refer patients. I respect anyone who can do the top 10% most complicated cases. It must be so rewarding to do the 10% others cannot. My hat goes off to all the specialists, for sure. I am simply saying from my experience, the specialists that are making the most typically encourage their general dentist friends to seek CE, support them and encourage them to perform these high-value procedures. Let's think abundantly and uplift one another.

Do good dentistry, invest in your dental CE
and buy advanced technology
so they will beat a path to your door

WRONG! This will only put you further in debt--UNLESS you do it at the right time for the right reasons. What do I mean by this?

Timing is very important in deciding when to invest in dental CE and technology.

For Example:

A start-up practice with a first-time owner or inexperienced clinician does not need a cone beam CT, laser and an in-house milling unit. A seasoned practice owner who has a profitable practice and is able to predict their ROI on the CE or technology based on the statistics and patient demographics of their office is a good candidate. These are two extreme examples, but I believe everyone reading can extrapolate the point.

How do you know when to buy the technology?

AVOID emotional purchases. We often buy because we geek out on the technology and its capabilities or because our peers or mentors are doing it or because someone sold us the idea that if we don't then we're a crappy dentist. Invest logically, not emotionally.

Base the introduction of technology on your current office capacity. Are you operating at 1% or 100% capacity? Base your decision on new patient volume, profit and production by procedure breakdown. For example, if you are considering a scanner/miller for crowns, ask yourself how many crowns you deliver each month and how many do you need to do to hit your break-even point? This will give you some insight to the right timing, demand and potential ROI. In addition, look at call conversion and treatment conversion numbers in addition to your collections percentage. WHY? Because investing in expensive technology before you have the basics of business down is a mistake.

I would never discourage anyone from getting more education. The goal of more CE should be on the forefront of every practitioners' mind. You want to begin taking courses early and for the rest of your career. Just take the right course at the right time for the right reason.

I love the quote by Frank Clark:

"The more you learn, the more you earn."

Although this holds true most of the time, the consistent execution of this knowledge is what earns you more money. You don't want to come out guns blazing taking every CE course marketed to you, in every treatment modality out there. I did this and it felt great. I felt significant but my ROI was low, and I wasn't prepared to apply even a fraction of the knowledge I'd gained. Look, if you have no budget limits, go crazy. If you do, be methodical about your approach by getting good at the basics: restorative, preventative, basic oral surgery and endo. Most thriving docs I have seen do 50-70% of their production from the basic "drill and fill" type procedures. The other 30-50% comes from more advanced procedures (practitioner level, not office level).

If you are thinking *I know a guy who has a practice limited to implants, cosmetics, or sleep*, I get it. I know those guys as well, and it's definitely possible, but it is the exception and requires much more work and upfront investment in education and technology to start. Please don't get caught up on exact percentages, as they may vary slightly. I am simply illustrating the point that the majority of patients want efficient, durable and relatively painless general dentistry and therefore there is something to be said about becoming proficient at this prior to investing thousands of dollars in more comprehensive and expensive programs

If you are reading this and are convinced you never want to do a root canal or an extraction, then begin taking CE in the areas in which you are interested. Perhaps you want to mainly or exclusively deliver high-value procedures such as ortho, implants or cosmetic dentistry. By all means, start learning early and get the ball rolling now. For those of you who are uncertain where to start and simply want to increase your competence, confidence and efficiency in the delivery of general dental procedures, invest in educating yourself in the most common procedures performed and learn to do those well.

As you begin to grow your offices or invest in CE, think about starting with a molar endo course and oral sedation OR oral/nitrous combo. This will allow you to grow and increase your bottom line without significant investment into a comprehensive ortho, implant or IV sedation program. There's nothing wrong with these, I have done tons of CE in all these areas myself. But again, timing is important--as is ROI!

I am an advocate for both technology and CE. Just remember to invest in CE and technology logically, not emotionally. There's nothing cool about spending 100K on a comprehensive implant program if you don't understand how to attract enough implant patients to get a decent ROI.

Here are some other tips:

- Take courses or programs online and locally to start (this will save you thousands of dollars).
- Take your staff to the CE program. If you can't afford to do so, put together a presentation on the topic to empower them with education. Their buy-in is important to your lead generation and case conversion.
- Calculate the number of procedures you will have to complete in order to recover your tuition costs
- Prior to attending the program, begin lining up patients in your practice so you can begin as soon as you return.
- Don't buy all the fancy gadgets for delivery of the newly learned procedure. Instead, ask your reps if you can borrow and try the technology out for the first few cases. Typically, you don't need the full-meal deal in order to do easy implant cases.
- Look for a local mentor or specialist who has excelled in an area you are interested in. Anyone

with an abundant mindset will be happy to help. Join a mastermind/study club.

VERY IMPORTANT: I don't discuss it here because the remainder of the book will give you a healthy dose of this advice. Invest as much in your leadership, management and business development training as you do into your dental CE. If you're not a do-it-yourself type in reference to business or you are looking to collapse time frames, learn from those ahead of you on the timeline and join a dental business mastermind or hire a coach/consultant who has produced results for others. I can't express enough how valuable it is for you to achieve your goals and create the lifestyle of which you dream. Hold off on the BMW, expensive dinners and vacations. Invest in yourself and you will grow your results by 10 times, paying you dividends for years to come.

Rapid debt reduction is not necessary

In my opinion, debt reduction should be a priority. I have had the good fortune to be friends with multi-millionaires and have met a few billionaires in my short career. I have learned tons of lessons from these people. One lesson in particular is to live below your means and stay liquid. For some of those colleagues, that still meant they were able to buy planes, trains and automobiles of their liking but they were spending significantly less than they earned. All of them were earning money, investing money and saving money simultaneously. They all recognized that debt was a necessary component of scaling their businesses, but they were strategic about the type of debt they took on. They made damned sure that if shit hit the fan they would be able protect themselves personally (creditor proof) or remain liquid enough to sustain the fallow season to come. Your goal may not be to be a millionaire or a billionaire, but the point is getting your money in order and ensure you do not take on unnecessary debt associated with luxury purchases both inside and outside your business.

One thing that saddens me is that the majority of dentists don't have enough money to retire by the age of 65 and continue to sustain the lifestyle to which they have become accustomed. I don't know about you, but I don't want to HAVE to go into work. I'm doing everything in my power now to ensure that if I decide to throw in the towel and lie on the beach 365 days a year, I'll have the freedom and choice to do so. I don't ever see that happening, as I would go insane and drive all those around me crazy. I need to be productive and see progress and growth in order to be satisfied with myself. But the point is, if I want to, I should be able to retire very comfortably.

Carrying significant personal or business debt will make this impossible for you. The future carries too much uncertainty with respect to health and well-being to guarantee an income until the age of 65. Living conservatively is the key. Of course, conservative is relative term. None of you are going to be eating Kraft boxed dinners every night, nor will you be living in a trailer park.

This path to freedom, as I define it, starts by getting your finances in order both personally and in your business. As you earn, you can begin to take excess funds in your business and partially reinvest it into your business, so it grows. Excess is defined as what you have after you have paid yourself what you need to live. You allocate part of your earnings and automate low-risk, long-term investments and savings. You can do all of this now. You don't need to be earning $1 million per year to do this.

In his book *Master the Game*, Tony Robbins tells the story of Theodore Johnson.

"Theodore Johnson worked for UPS and never made more than $14,000 a year, and yet, in his old age, he was worth more than $70 million. When he said he had no money to save, a friend told him that if he were taxed, the money would be taken out of his account and he'd never see it. So, he created a tax for himself to make him wealthy. Even though he made little money, he took 20 percent of his money and it went straight into an investment account. Over more than five decades, that compounded to make him $70 million."

I am not an expert in investments, I am simply sharing with you what I have learned from those who are experts. Some people may say their accountant or tax advisor says they can afford to spend $X or they suggested they keep their business debt and student loan debt around for a number of years. Some may suggest they consolidate and refinance their student loan debt when they purchase their practice and other comments like that.

I recommend if you trust your advisers, you follow their advice as long as they can demonstrate to you their logic and you can measure their results. My experience has been that rapid debt reduction trumps all tax planning strategies that utilize debt to reduce taxes, and it carries less risk. The more liquid you are, the more money you can invest and save. Compound interest is a great thing. You will learn to love it more each year. If you are one of those saying, "*Screw that. I didn't go to school for eight years and bust my ass so I can be conservative. I want to live my dream life now,*" I understand where you are coming from. I did that for three years before I began following the advice in this book. It cost me a fortune and I had to work twice as hard simply to keep my head above water. No judgment on my end. Everyone should live life on their terms, and if that means spending everything you earn and more in pursuit of happiness and pleasure from material items and lavish experiences then you should do that. It's important that you do what you feel is best for you. I chose to do things differently now and I am only sharing this with you so you are aware of an alternative view.

Dental practices only fail 1% of the time

Define failure for me, please?

This is unique to each person. I define failure in private practice as owning a practice that does not afford the dentist both the money and the free time they desire. With respect to the 1% failure rate thrown around quite often, I suspect that while they may not go belly up and close their doors, they may face other problems such as the following:

- Is the dentist working 80 hours per week to keep their doors open?
- Is sustaining the practice causing so much stress the dentist is numbing themselves with food, drugs or alcohol?
- Is the dentist able to spend time with their family? Are they divorced? Do they have time for the most important people and partnerships in their life (kids and spouse)?
- Is the dentist dipping into their personal income in order to pay their business expenses and amortize debt? ~Are they taking as much money home as they would like or are they working for basically three times minimum wage?
- Has the practice exchanged hands multiple times or is the dentist holding the debt/note while someone else has stepped in to run their office?
- Is the dentist mentally and physically healthy?

The point is, I don't know how this stat was calculated. It doesn't matter, because even if it is true that less than 1% of offices close their doors and the failure rate is in fact that low, it depends on your definition of failure.

What I want for dentists is a practice which gives them both time and money. I am not saying they won't have to put in the long hours and make sacrifices. That is the nature of business. But I am saying that a strategic approach to running your business will result in achievement and success as I define it once you have a well-oiled machine.

Practice Ownership is for Everyone and Owning a Practice is Your Ticket to Freedom

In the words of Napoleon Hill, author of *Think and Grow Rich"*

"The mind can achieve whatever it can conceive and believe."

I wholeheartedly believe this, and this is why I believe anyone who wants to be a practice owner and is all-in can be a practice owner and should be a practice owner. But I also believe that practice ownership is not for everyone, just like entrepreneurship isn't for all business graduates. The reason I have developed this belief is through observation. I think a lot of doctors decide to seek practice ownership for the wrong reasons. Practice ownership may be inconsistent with their values, beliefs and desired lifestyle. That doesn't mean they can't do it. It just means maybe they should think twice about it and ensure this is truly what they want. Think about what practice ownership really entails:

- *Heavy Responsibilities* - You will have financial commitments that you personally guarantee, such as lease agreements and equipment purchases. Team management, marketing and liability are all major responsibilities tied to owning your practice.

- *Potentially Low and Unpredictable Income* - The practice owner is often the last person to get paid--if they get paid at all, in early days. Payroll and rent take priority, leading to more than a few sleepless nights. It is not for the faint of heart.

- *Need for Business Education* - Being a dentist is not enough to run a successful practice. Practice owners must get an education on how to run a business in addition to becoming a dentist.

- *Faux Freedom* - Practice ownership does not come with the freedom you might think it does. Practice owners do decide where to spend their time, but the consequences are so high, it really isn't a choice.

IMPORTANT NOTE: You can create this over time, but it takes leadership, great office culture, a reliable team and systems to allow for freedom. Even then, you will need to install habits and rituals to ensure when you are away from the practice you are able to disconnect and be present in the moment and enjoy your life! Some are great at disconnecting. I certainly am not, but rigid routines help me get there.

Practice Ownership is the Fastest Path to Paying Off Debt

This can be true depending on the circumstances. Below are some very basic factors to consider. It is not a comprehensive list, just food for thought.

Start-up Considerations

What is the dentist to patient population ratio or demographics, such as in-migration, median income, insured vs. un-insured, etc.? As important as a demographic study is a competitive analysis. For example, will the new practice be located in an area where all the dentists are aggressively marketing and providing comprehensive dental services (AKA: super GP's) or can the new dentist out-market or out-procedure their competitors?

Is the practitioner experienced or a new grad? It is great to be located in an area where new patient influx will be high. However, one must factor in their diagnostic abilities and skill level, as well. Having multiple new patients come in the front door only to leave out the back door is not a profitable growth model.

Does the owner understand how to grow or sustain a practice? If they don't, have they budgeted for training in this area or the fees for a coach or consultant?

Acquisition Considerations

Consider the above in addition to:

- Is it profitable and is the new owner able to step in and replicate the production?
- Has appropriate due diligence taken place to confirm profitability (tax returns/P&L's)?

The acquisitions I did that caused the greatest operational and growth challenges were the under-performing, under-procedured, under-marketed offices with high overhead and little profit which we purchased at a bargain. I suggest purchasing profitable offices in which you can replicate the production easily. The key here is not to pay a huge premium.

I have completed five acquisitions and four start-ups. Each mistake was painful and definitely cost me, delaying my growth and progress. My passion for business, great mentors, great partners and hustle allowed me to create profitable operations out of all but one of these. That's a story for another time. (Let's just say embezzlement and a dysfunctional partnership may have been a factor!)

The bottom line is this--practice ownership is not always the fastest path to paying off your debt. Davidson suggests that it takes the average business start-up two-to-three years to become profitable[i]. Dental practices are not immune, especially when you consider the capital requirements and unreliable cash flows. How do you think you can afford to pay off student loans quicker if payroll and office rent continue to drain your bank account?

You're more likely to increase your debt when you own a practice. Operating lines of credit, equipment loans and office leases are all debt requirements for which you are on the hook. If you are considering purchasing a practice, it may be in your best interest to work with a successful practice owner and take tons of notes before you take the plunge. In this process, you may decide you don't want to do it, or on the other hand, that you have gained enough information to do it well. Either way, this will benefit you. Another option is a strategic partnership. Partner One wears the business hat and Partner Two wears the dentist hat and they both live happily ever after. I recognize finding the right strategic partner is the key and I am not suggesting you get into bed with just anyone.

The Million Dollar Practice Owner You Admire is Healthy, Wealthy and Living the Dream

Most other practice owners don't want to admit, openly, at least, that they are super stressed out about managing their own practices. Few openly share what kind of work it actually takes to earn the income they do.

So many are free in sharing that their practice grosses $1 million, but that's not how much they make. Owning a practice is not about how much money your business makes. It's about how much money *you* get to keep. I have participated in mastermind groups with business owners generating $50-100M in annual revenue and yet are not profitable. They are the CEOS of $100M dollar companies who openly share they are a few bad moves away from having to close their doors. The CEOs I am talking about shared openly with the group, asked for help, received it and went on to not only grow their companies, but generate significant profit and wealth. It all started with them being vulnerable and honest about the current state of their businesses. It is okay to admit you're not profitable and ask for help.

More important than money is time. How much time does their practice afford them? Few practice owners who net a sizable profit have the time to enjoy it with those they care about. Their practice becomes a black hole for their time and requires every waking moment to generate an income. Success, at least by my standards, gives dentists both money AND time.

We are being sold a dream but are only given half of the details. Other practice owners may be happy to share all the glory they enjoy. They have a great income or lifestyle. Rarely do they share the grind they have to go through to get those things--the 18-hour days, working weekends to keep up with administration work, sleepless nights and the constant threat of competition.

In part, society perpetuates this embellished self-reporting.

Earning any professional designation has a ton of social value but none higher than that of a dentist or doctor. You gain immediate status when you become a dentist. Most people feel the lifestyle of a dentist is pretty good. The profession has this stigma attached to it. We are expected to be rich. If we are not, we don't like to tell anyone, so we spend above our means in an effort to maintain the image. Your degree does not guarantee you a great lifestyle. It simply provides you with an opportunity to do so. The rest is about learning, execution and grit.

I am not judging anyone. I *was* this guy until I changed my way of thinking and realized I needed to spend less time talking about how sexy practice ownership is by inflating my results and being more forthcoming with myself and everyone around me. This level of real talk and truth sets you free and allows you to begin finding solutions to the problems. You can then begin to legitimately boast, although I don't recommend it. Instead, help others to find the same success.

If You Need to Market Your Practice, You're not a Great Dentist.

Most doctors I interact with understand that consistent marketing efforts are a requirement to generate new patients for their practices. Others invest intermittently or when they subjectively feel they need new patients. This is typically when revenue declines for a few consecutive months. Others believe it's only for those practitioners who are unethical or swindling. There are only a few of these people remaining. The chances are those doctors aren't reading this book or attending the conferences I am. This level of thinking is old-school.

A mentor of mine taught me you must think and behave like a marketer if you plan on creating a successful business. Think of yourself as a marketing agency that just happens to deliver dental services.

Corporate Dentistry is Ruining Your Chances of Becoming a Profitable Practice Owner

Corporate dentistry has some advantages which include but are not limited to the following:

- Recruitment of talent through provision of incentives.
- Training and continuing education.
- Economies of scale (compete on price).
- Marketing directors.
- Centralized services to ensure cash flow and operations are optimized

I agree well-run corporate practices have the ability to outcompete you, but it is not a certainty. If you have an existing patient base, great customer service and patient retention strategies, an awesome office culture, happy staff and systems to ensure your marketing and management of people, time and money are tight, you will have a huge advantage. The challenge is that many practitioners are either stuck in a rut of practicing and managing like they always have and are unwilling to change their ways or don't have the knowledge or experience to operate as well as their corporate competitors. The corporate players don't consider the single owner operator a threat. It's time for you to begin thinking in the same way. Work ON the business and your worries will decrease substantially. Bottom line: Build a great business and you have nothing to worry about.

***

As you make your way through the remainder of the book, I suggest taking notes and getting through the entire book before beginning to implement anything you've learned. The content in the book is significant and may at times seem overwhelming. Don't worry about that at first, just read and move on. After finishing the book, you can circle back to the chapters which were most relevant to you and do deeper dives.

My hope is that by reading this book, you will be able to learn some tools and tactics to take your practice to the next level. Another hope is that if you are currently running a declining or stagnant practice, you now know what it means to run a successful one, and you will seek a strategic partner or mentor to help you climb to the top. Lastly, I hope this may help you decide whether practice ownership is for you.

Dentistry is an amazing industry and provides a great career to everyone who chooses their paths thoughtfully. I wish you tremendous success in life both personally and professionally.

CHAPTER TWO

Why

"The two most important days in life are
the day you are born and the day
you discover the reason why."
~Mark Twain

This quote has so much meaning for me. By the time you are finished reading this chapter and this book, I hope Mark Twain's words will have just as much meaning for you. You have experienced at least one of the most important days of your life. Have you discovered your reason why?

That is going to be the hardest question I will ask you and it will be the toughest one for you to answer. Many people go through their entire lives with an empty feeling from having not discovered the reason why. So, let's lighten this up a little bit, then.

Why are you reading this book? Are you frustrated with dentistry, running your practice or both? Perhaps you are dissatisfied with your success level thus far? Or maybe you're doing well but you're not feeling fulfilled. Or you are stressed? Maybe you are doing well but want to take things to the next level. Or maybe you are an associate or dental student looking to become a practice owner.

In this book you are going to get answers to all of the above and more. But I have to caution you before you continue on. I am going to challenge you to think differently!

You can expect a balanced mix of left-brain discussions about strategies, tools, tactics and metrics combined with right-brain soft skills and personal/professional development requirements to build a high-performance practice.

This book is not for you if:

- You have little ambition to build a high-performance practice.
- You are unwilling to expand out of your comfort zone and take action that may scare you.
- You are closed minded to the fact that you don't know everything.
- You are not willing to internalize the content in these pages and take massive, immediate action to make improvement.
- You don't believe or are unwilling to even consider that a dental practice is a business.

If this is you, then no need to continue reading. I wish you all the best and invite you back when you are ready.

This book is definitely for you if:

- You want to have more, be more, do more and give more.
- You are ready to bust through your comfort zone.
- You are prepared to do what it takes to build a business that affords you the lifestyle you deserve, desire or of which you dream.

***

Think back to when you first decided to pursue your profession and enter dental school. You knew it wasn't going to be easy. You must have had some profound reason to begin your education and the pursuit of the professional you are today. Didn't you?
That reason was so powerful that it got you through all of the late nights, massive stress, tough exams and lengthy papers. Maybe you ate ramen noodles for two years to be able to afford to go to school. That's a pretty powerful *why* to keep you going through all of that stress and heartache. To finish and not quit.

What was that *why*? Did you decide to do it for yourself? To prove to yourself that you could do it and were worthy of it? Perhaps you did it to prove something to others. Maybe you held an old grudge, somebody told you that you couldn't do it, and you decided to put your head down and get it done to prove them wrong.

You might even be on a journey to find significance. Maybe that's why you decided to pursue your profession.

Perhaps your *why* is something as simple as money. Maybe lifestyle is why you've decided to pursue your profession. You want to live in a certain way, live in a particular home, drive a specific car, eat in nice restaurants and take luxury vacations. You've pursued one of the highest-paid professions in the world and there is no shame in earning a high income as a result of all the education and skill you have acquired.

Or maybe your *why* is a little more altruistic than that, and you wanted to pursue your career to help others. Maybe you want to help others become healthier.

Perhaps your *why* is a little bit of all of the above.

Without a profound *why*, there is a high likelihood failure will ensue and people either quit, self-destruct, lose fulfillment or become jaded or bitter. Scaling a business and growing your dental practice is no easy task. There will be plenty of obstacles along the way. A profound *why* will help you learn from these challenges, dust yourself off and move upward and onward. Without it, we often question why the heck we are putting ourselves through this intense stress and often succumb to the pressure. This shows up in multiple forms, but most often as poor mental/physical heath, relationships and finances.

When I decided to become a dentist, my *why* was a little bit of all of the above. I didn't grow up in a wealthy household. I saw my Dad work really, really hard throughout his entire life. In spite of that, he had people who were not as smart as he was being more successful financially and getting further ahead in life.

My Mom always valued education. It's one of the many values that she taught me. She always said that getting a good education would:

- set me free
- get me respect
- buy me freedom
- make life easier

I remember times when we had to take groceries out of the cart because we didn't have enough money in the bank to be able to pay for them. Multiple uncomfortable experiences similar to these drove me to want to abolish this issue from my life.

One of my profound *whys* is money and lifestyle. There is a certain freedom which comes with the lifestyle of a dentist and/or business owner. The pursuit of doing what I want, when I want and with whom I want appeals to me. For me it's not specifically about the money, but rather what the money can do for me.
Being successful in a profession which pays well has changed the course of my family forever. It has also allowed me to provide for my team and my community. So, in a way, I am also doing it for others.

But here's my biggest *why*:

I want to be a great leader--being an example for my children and showing them how to be successful instead of just telling them how I think they may be successful.

I want to have a positive impact on other people and be able to help them in ways that very few other people can help them. Two of my most important values (aside from my family and health) is becoming a global influencer and being my best self. Without sounding too cliché, I am on a perpetual journey of progress and growth. I want absolutely no regrets on my proverbial deathbed. I also want that for you.

Owning a business enables me to solve problems and the more problems I solve, the more people I help. When I help more people, I have a greater impact. The greater my impact, the more my income continues to grow. All of these, in that order, have attracted the business and the lifestyle of my dreams. Money follows value. Value comes from impact. The impact starts with giving others what they need to progress, grow and live the life of their dreams. The money is simply a report card for me. If your making more money it means you're having a greater impact. As well, I believe your income reflects your identity and in order to earn more you need to become more. Most important is who I am becoming in this process.

A big question to answer is--are you doing this for yourself or is your *why* because you want to do this for others? Perhaps you're after significance, money or lifestyle. Or maybe, if your story is just a little bit like mine, you want all of the above, and that's the *why* which drives you.

"What you do speaks so loudly,
I can't hear what you're saying."
~Ralph Waldo Emerson

Did you know that most doctors, dentists and other professionals don't see their practice as a business? Though many will talk about being an entrepreneur, their actions will tell me all I need to know. If you plan to become a "practice" owner you must see yourself as a "business" owner.

Michael Gerber, in his book *The E-Myth*, talks about a major misconception people have when they go into business--not after they go into business but before, prior to experiencing what he calls the "entrepreneurial seizure", which is the prevalence of thoughts and beliefs that becoming an entrepreneur will give you everything you've ever dreamed of. It will give you the freedom you desire, allow you to be your own boss and ultimately the master of your domain. "Most business owners were typically working for someone else or doing technical work prior to adopting these new beliefs. They were a hairdresser, a technical writer, an accountant, a doctor or a [dentist]. Whatever they were, they were likely doing technical work. But the most disastrous and fatal assumption made was: if you understand the technical work of a business you understand a business that does that technical work. The reason it's fatal is it just isn't true. In fact, it's the root cause of most small business failures. The technical work of a business and the business that does the technical work are two totally different things. But the technician who starts the business fails to see this. To the technician suffering from an entrepreneurial seizure a business is not a business but a place to go to work. So, the technician becomes a business owner, believing by understanding the technical work of the business [Example: the provision of dental services], they are immediately and imminently qualified to run the business that does that kind of work--and that's simply not true."

Dentistry is a business!

Do you currently own your own office or multiple facilities? If so, why did you choose to become a business owner? If not, why do you want to be a business owner?

When I got into dental school and then finally graduated, I felt I had made it. I thought I was done, I was there, and I was going to be living a great life. But what I didn't realize was that my education was just a ticket to the game. I had imagined that dentistry was the path to get me all of those things that I wanted.

In dental school, I recognized most of my full-time professors were either failing in private practice or truly passionate about academics, so they decided to take a teaching position. On the other hand, the part-time guys who came into the clinic floor were either there to take out their anger on the students and make them feel inferior or uplift and inspire them.

The inspirational up-lifters were the ones to whom I was attracted and who comforted me. These professors were the ones with whom I began forming relationships. I discovered these ladies and gentlemen were crushing it in their private practices. They were routinely outperforming their peers and happier for it. I asked them lot of questions and learned a ton. I will be forever grateful to these early dental mentors.

They also taught me that my clinical skills were only one predictor of my success in private practice. It was my ability to run a business that ultimately would triumph. They all encouraged me to improve my dental skills and knowledge, but also to invest in practice management and development. I loved business as much as I loved dentistry from the get-go, so they didn't have to tell me twice. This motivated me to seek more information.

Prior to graduating dental school, I sent out 1000 letters to 1000 dental offices across north America with an approximately 10% response rate. 100% of those doctors were willing to get on the phone with me or allow me to meet with them in person. I set out on my journey to interview these doctors and prepared a list of questions. What I learned was that the top producers, the most fulfilled, and the doctors who were still married and happy to show up to return to their homes each night, had several traits in common. They got their money right. They understood that a profitable practice was a huge priority and did everything in their control to create one. They understood that the path to a profitable practice was understanding business AND dentistry; not just one or the other. Some of them did it on their own. Others chose to form strategic partnerships where one partner focused on the business and the other dentistry. Either way, they achieved highly profitable and efficient operations that afforded them the lifestyle they desired.

After all of this learning, what did I do? I tried to keep everything in balance for the first few years. I invested in coaches, consultants and practice management programs in addition to taking continuing education in all facets of dentistry--totaling hundreds of hours each year to increase my competence. The end result was an increase in my confidence, which enabled me to increase my career satisfaction and enrich my patients' lives.
My second year was similar. I worked on my dental skills and continued investing in my education. To this day I invest in myself and will continue to do so for my lifetime.

"The most important investment you can make is in yourself."
- Warren Buffet

In spite of all the preparation and education, I still failed in my execution multiple times. I have probably failed more in the first part of my career than many have failed in their lifetime. I certainly didn't have everything figured out in the beginning. I didn't execute flawlessly. The information was great, but the game is execution. I failed many times, but I didn't quit. I learned and moved on quickly. I pivoted fast and course corrected often. This process of learning, failing well and quickly moving on allowed me to get new patients in the door, retain them, create multiple seven-figure practices (all highly profitable) and positively impact my team, patients and our local communities!

In order to practice dentistry, we first commit to an average of eight years of school. Then we have to spend another five years to get good clinically and also begin to develop leadership, management and marketing skills. The realization that it's almost a 13-year journey to create a successful and profitable office made me think--this is a lifetime commitment to continued learning and progress to stay ahead of the curve. All of that time had better pay off, because there are many other ways to make great money over 13 years.

Those eight-years of education is just a ticket to the game. You're really only sitting in the nosebleeds, when your goal should be sitting at the tenth row of the 50-yardline.

You see, being a good dentist wasn't enough. It's all the soft skills that made me really successful.

My patients don't necessarily know if I am a good dentist or not. I do good dentistry for my own satisfaction and believe I deserve the fee I charge as a good dentist. All they know is that their experience was quick, painless, durable and didn't break the bank. As well, they know, like and trust me. The key to building trust is good non-verbal and verbal communication.

As dentists, we all value doing great work, but few of us value becoming great communicators, leaders and business owners. I have observed that a perfectly competent dentist who can't talk to people or lead people does not have a successful practice.

As a dentist or practice owner, what business are you really in? You are in the relationship business, and all successful relationships are based on trust and excellent communication.

My wake-up calls have come in many shapes and forms throughout my journey. One time early in my career, I had an assistant come up to me and say, *"Your patients don't understand what you are saying to them. They are leaving confused because you're talking over them."* That's when I realized a dentist's job is to connect with people and explain things in ways they can understand clearly, as much as it is to do good work and help them get healthy. Educating patients in a way they can understand is a key component of value generation. It is important to understand that value generation plays a big role in treatment conversion.

Again, one massive question I would like to ask and have you answer for yourself is--why are you even interested in business? Please do not make the mistake of thinking you are not a business owner or an entrepreneur. Dentists tend to be absent CEO's. In other words, a dentist spends more time working in their clients' mouths and not on their business. It is not surprising, because that is how we were trained--to work on our craft. We have been sold the idea that if we become excellent clinicians the money will take care of itself. The problem is that an entrepreneur or business owner can EITHER be working *IN* their business or *ON* their business, but not both at the same time. How much time do you want to spend doing each?

Perhaps owning your own practice isn't for you right now. Maybe finding a strategic partner is more suitable, or maybe being a lifetime associate is right for you. By the time you are finished reading this book, you will gain the perspective you need to make that decision.

Whether you own multiple practices and have many employees and tons of patients, or you're a practitioner with one employee, you are a business owner.

So why are you even interested in business?

Are you clear on your *why*?

As Stephen Covey wrote in his book *Seven Habits of Highly Effective People*,

"Begin with the end in mind."

Imagine the lifestyle you want to have and everything you want to achieve, and then think backwards and reverse engineer your *why*. When you first decide your lifestyle, then you can build the business that brings that to fruition, because the emotion that comes when you think about that lifestyle underlies your *why*.

Your *why*, your lifestyle, dreams and purpose is unique to you! It doesn't have to be absolutely out of this world or one single thing. You can't rent someone else's dreams. Remember what leadership guru and best-selling author Robin Sharma says.

> *"Run your own race" Who cares what others are doing? The only question that matters is am I progressing?*

Think about the lifestyle you want to have. The house you want to live in, the car you want to drive, the types of vacations you want to take, the amount of time you'd like to volunteer, the charities you would like to support, the people on whom you would like to have a positive impact, the gifts you'd like to buy and the total amount of time off you'd like to take annually.

Ask yourself WHY? Why do I want these things? Do you desire significance, want to provide for your family, become your best self or positively impact others? Draw from within or use the information I have provided in this chapter. This why will keep you going when you hit roadblocks in your journey. Refer back to it to remind yourself why you signed up for this process in the first place.

Take massive action and begin implementing the steps required to build the business of your dreams. This part requires well-defined business goals, a road map or strategic plan to achieve them and consistent execution until the goals are achieved.

This final point will become clear as you read through this book. You will begin to identify areas that need improvement and you can use those to set your goals.

Ideas to Remember

- Why did you become a dentist?
- Your dental practice is a business.
- Why do you want to be a business owner?
- Do not rent someone else's dream/goals. Your *why* must be authentic and unique to you so it can be powerful enough to build a successful practice over the long-term
- Money is a tool. It's not about the money, but rather what the money can do.
- Reverse engineer your *why*. Decide what you want and ask yourself why you want it.

CHAPTER THREE

You Can't Manage What You Can't Measure

"Every line is the perfect length if you don't measure it."
~Marty Rubin

If you don't have any data, it's very difficult to pursue objective moves. Without data, it stands to reason that every decision becomes emotional and reactive. Every business, especially professional practices, will have difficulty managing without measuring against the industry's key performance indicators.

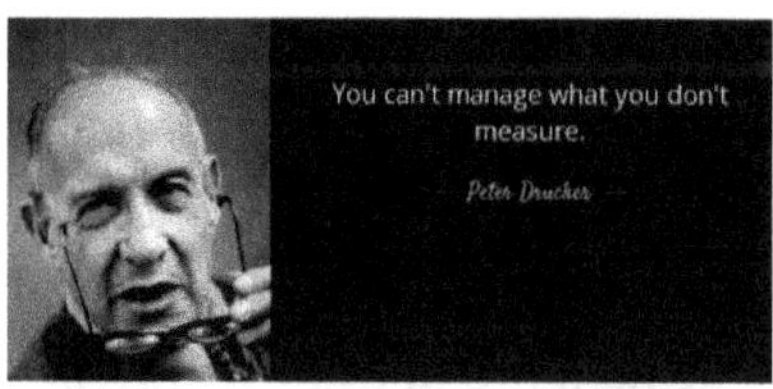

You can't manage what you don't measure.
Peter Drucker

Using Key Performance Indicators (KPI's) is the difference between growing a business-by-design versus a business-by-default. A business by design has control over performance despite uncontrollable circumstances. A business by default simply reacts to the uncontrollable circumstances, which often leads to failure.

I love what Marty Rubin says about every line being perfect if you don't measure. I thought it was the perfect lead-in to this chapter. How will you know if you are making progress towards fulfilling your purpose if you don't measure and have tangible references for success and failure?

In other words, if you don't measure your progress, it doesn't much matter where you are headed. It's just like the scene from Alice in Wonderland when Alice asks the Cheshire Cat which way she should go. The Cheshire Cat says it depends on where she wants to get to, but Alice says she doesn't care. Do you remember the Cheshire Cat's response? He says, "Then it doesn't much matter which way you go."

This chapter focuses on the measurements you need to manage the operation of your practice.
Before we dive in deeper, it's time to change your thinking. Sort of. I should say it is time to change parts of the way you think. If you are at all like me, when I came out of school and became a licensed dentist, I only ever viewed people as patients. It's not surprising, because this

is how we have been trained in professional school. We are trained that way at conferences, by product providers, colleagues, continuing education and so on. Just look at the Oxford definition for *patient*:

A person receiving or registered to receive medical treatment. This is very plain and dictates how we as medical professionals should behave when working with patients.

We absolutely have a moral and professional obligation to treat patients honestly and ethically, and running a business should never compromise this. We are enriching the lives of patients through the provision of our services. The interesting thing is, many successful and fulfilled entrepreneurs and business owners I have met do the same with their clients. That is, they are honest, ethical and enrich their clients' lives. The bottom line is we serve our patients, who then pay for our services. By that logic, patients are also clients.

This is where I would like to challenge you. I am going to ask you to shift the way you think about patients. In addition to considering patients as those receiving dental treatment, I want you to stretch just a little bit and think about your patients as people receiving services. People who have a choice of providers for those services. When people have a choice where to spend their time and money for products and services, they can also be viewed as clients or customers. Have you ever thought about your patients as clients or customers?

Learning this early on from mentors allowed me to understand how to deliver great customer service from the get-go. I understood my patients are clients who have choices about which dentist they choose to treat them, and which treatment plans they will allow us to complete. I understood that in addition to my career as a dentist, I am ALSO a business owner. This level of thinking led me to acquire, build and manage several seven-figure practices. I think of myself as dentist AND a business owner.

Throughout the rest of the book, I will refer to your dental practice as your dental business and your patients as clients. These words will be used interchangeably.

Dental Practice = Dental Business

Patients = Clients

There are no written words to describe how important it was for me to think of myself as a business owner as much as a dentist. This is also why I am sharing this with you. I want you to have all success you've ever dreamed of in whatever form that takes for you. I want you to achieve success and fulfillment in every aspect of your life. Remember the last chapter where we had a lengthy discussion about your *why*? I want you to keep that in mind for the remainder of the book. Always come back to that.

If you are thinking, *Yeah, yeah, yeah, I understand my practice is a business and I treat it as such.* GREAT! If not, the first step you must take is to view patients as people with choices. In other words, you must also consider them clients.

> *Learning Lesson*
> *Do you know the difference between a customer and a client?*
>
> *An interaction with a customer is transactional Neither are heavily invested in the relationship and the interaction is over once the transaction is complete.*
>
> *A client relationship requires investment from both parties with an interest in a continuing relationship. A fruitful client will likely lead to repeat business or qualified referrals.*

Three Ways to Grow a Business

I am a big fan of Jay Abraham. If you haven't heard of him, do a quick Google search and you will find a ton of information about him. He has written some amazing books like *The Sticking Point Solution* and *Getting Everything You Can Out of All You've Got*, among others. He's an accomplished speaker and is highly-sought-after as a business consultant. One of the most important lessons I have learned from Jay is that there are only three ways to grow a business. I know. I was surprised to hear that, too.

The only three ways to grow a business:

- **Attract new clients.**

Translation: External marketing campaigns and internal referrals to generate more new patients whom you can potentially convert to long-term clients.

- **Increase the average transaction value per client.**

Translation: Comprehensive treatment plans, effective treatment presentations to increase case acceptance, and high value procedures such as implants, orthodontics, cosmetic dentistry, periodontal surgery and sleep apnea treatments.

- **Increase the average transaction frequency per client.**

Translation: Effective follow up appointments and appropriate hygiene frequency with three, four, six, nine or 12-month recalls. Comprehensive periodontal program focused on oral systemic health is one example of how frequency can be increased.

In the simplest of terms, you can get more new people to buy something from you, increase the amount they buy from you or increase the number of times they buy from you. The most powerful part of this lesson is to compound all three!

One more thing you need to understand before we move forward:

Sell More
Spend Less

Here are the three ways a business makes money: sell more, spend less or do both. Profit is the spread between the revenue and expenses. The wider the gap, the higher the gain. Over the rest of this chapter you will find a deep dive into important metrics required to run a successful practice. Just a warning--some of the discussion will include sales.

There is no way around the sales function. There shouldn't be. What needs to change is our perception of the sales role. As you continue to read, keep that in mind.

The path to *Sell More, Spend Less* starts with the Profit & Loss (P&L) statement. The success of your practice depends on it.

Your practice is either

- Growing
- Stagnating
- Failing

The first indication of where your practice falls will come from your Profit & Loss statement, or statement of income and retained earnings. The numbers don't lie. They are objective, not subjective. It's not about how much money you make. It's about how much money you *keep*. If you want to keep more of your hard-earned money, pay attention to the numbers.

According to the Small Business Administration (SBA),[ii] only 50% of businesses make it five years. That's a staggering number of failures. I have found that the P&L offers all the signs of failure before it happens. The numbers tell a story even if we cannot see it for ourselves. I would even go so far to say that while dental offices may not fail as often as the average small business, it is still important to track your numbers.

Often I speak with other dentists and they boast that their practice is grossing over $1MM. That is a nice accomplishment, but my next question is: How much does your practice net?

My philosophy is that it's not how much money you make that matters. It is how much money you *keep* and how much time you have. Those are the important numbers. Now, back to discussing whether your practice is growing, stagnating or failing. It is your P&L (Profit & Loss statement) which will tell that story. The KPI's (Key Performance Indicators) we will discuss in this chapter are just some of the measures I use to evaluate the performance of my practices.

I have two methods to measure performance--Benchmarks and Trends

The *benchmark* measurement is compared to a specific performance standard. These types of measurements can either be evaluated as a dollar amount or as a percentage. Wages are a great example. You create a specific monthly budget for wages that you benchmark or measure your wages as a percentage of revenue, for example no more than 25%. Wages will include all bonuses, benefits, incentives and payroll (salaried and hourly, regional variations apply).

Trend performance measures are tracked over time and are used to compare different time periods. These measures tell you how well your business is improving or identify areas that need attention. When you look at your bank statement at the end of the month and you don't have enough money left over to do payroll, you probably ought to take just a weekend to determine where all this money is going so you can make a course-correction.

How do you know when your practice is performing well? The obvious answer is when you are living the lifestyle you want or are at least on track to get there. The other answer is to compare your practice to the top 5%.

You may or may not want to build a business that compares with the top 5%. Whatever your dream is for your practice, those are the measures you need to hit to build the practice you want.

Here is a list of just a few important Key Performance Indicators you should measure in your practice:

Patient KPI's	Expenses	Revenue	Other
New Patient Flow	Consumables	Billing per hour/doctor	Collection Rate
Patient Attrition	Lab Expenses	Billing per hour/hygienist	Daily Break Even
Re-Appointment Rate	Wages		Cost per Procedure
Treatment Conversion			# Days to Next New Patient Availability
No Shows (%)			

The list of measures you may use your business is endless. It is up to you to decide which measures are important for your practice.

Leading vs. Lagging

A quick discussion about Leading vs. Lagging indicators. A leading indicator is a predictive measurement, while a lagging indicator is an output measurement.

Leading indicators are predictive. In other words, changes in a leading indicator, such as new patient flow, will result in a change in one or more outputs, like revenue. These are important measures because they are in-process measures.

Lagging indicators are results or outputs. Revenue and expenses are examples of after-event (in the past) measurements (hence the lagging).

You have more control or influence over leading indicators, even though they can be more difficult to measure. You have less (or sometimes no) control over lagging indicators, but their measures are specific and objective. The lagging indicators show where there are opportunities to improve, but the changes will come in processes measured by leading indicators.

Your job as a dentist, professional or small business owner is to figure out the important lead indicators and their relationship to the result or lagging indicators.

Collection Percentage

A business needs profit to grow, but cash flow to survive. It can operate for a considerable time without profit, but it will not last long without cash flow. Your collection percentage directly affects your cash flow.

For instance, your practice may have generated $80,000 in revenue last month. If your total expenses were $60,000 then your net profit is $20,000. This profit does not necessarily mean net real cash flow.
Collection percentage is a lagging indicator flagging that something is broken in your process. My benchmark for collection percentage is 97% or higher. Anything below that and I know something is not working properly and my practice is leaking cash.

I hear many doctors talk about how well their offices are doing and boast about their production. My follow-up question is, "What is your collections percentage?" The key figure is the total amount collected that ends up in the bank as opposed to simply what you produced.

Now that you have something you can measure, it can be managed. Here are some reasons your collection percentage may be low:

Falling Behind on Processing Insurance Payments and Checks.

One big flaw in your process is when your team delays processing insurance payments and checks. You need to find out why the delays are happening, starting with communication. Is it possible your team members do not see the urgency in processing these payments as they arise? Perhaps this is the task they put off until they complete all of their other tasks. Perhaps the hold-up is caused by delayed mail pickup or any other of a list of hundreds of possibilities. The point is, the measure indicates there is a problem. The good news is this can be easily identified and corrected.

Not Collecting Co-Payments

Neglecting to collect co-payments is another issue that should be corrected. This matter may be a little more involved depending on the source of the problem. You may find out that members of your team do not know which appointments and services require a co-payment, or perhaps they feel uncomfortable asking for the payment. In either case, and many others, this problem can be corrected through training.

Payment Plans

Although payment plans will have an impact on your collection percentage, they aren't necessarily an indication that your practice is leaking cash. Payment plans impact your cash flow because you are performing a service today and being paid for it later. An example is when you perform a $2500 service and agree to finance the fee for $100 per month for 25 months (assuming no finance charge). You are effectively recovering 4% ($100/$2500) every month until all the payments are made. This only applies if you are doing in-house financing or procedures such as orthodontics, in which patients pay monthly until the payments are complete. I advocate using a third party that will pay you in full and handle the payments for the treatment on your behalf, so this is never an issue for you.

Learning Lesson

Payment plans cause a delay in your cashflow, which carries some risk of default, as well as opportunity cost (somewhere else you could have used those funds). You can include a finance charge in your payment plans to offset that risk.

Point of Sale (POS) financing is another source of immediate cashflow that will increase your collection percentage. In POS financing, a finance company will pay you the price of the approved service less a fee and then collect monthly payments from the client.

Embezzlement

Embezzlement is a very difficult problem to diagnose and remedy. It can dramatically affect your collection percentage. You must tread warily here. Collection percentage is not the only indicator of embezzlement. You may be meeting your expected targets and you may still be leaking cash because of embezzlement. You may require a third party to investigate and audit your cash flow. When you do confirm that someone has been stealing, act immediately. First, contact your lawyer and consult with your trusted human resources adviser. There are multiple ways you can reduce the risk of embezzlement in your office.

Here are some quick tips:

- Criminal record check for all employees
- Check references and speak to last employer

- Be wary of team members asking for cash advances or early paydays
- Don't leave one person in charge of the finances (split the role)
- Print an audit trail daily from your practice management software
- Receive visa and checking account statements at your home
- Review adjustments and question them
- Be concerned about employees with personal issues, potential drug abuse problems and those who refuse to take time off or share their role with other team members

Processing Lag

One important note for you to remember is how lag can affect your collection percentage. Lag is simply the timing differences between when the treatments are performed and when the payments are processed.

Lag can occur when your billing cycles with insurance companies are out of sync with their payment schedules. Lag can also happen when treatments are performed near the end of the month and payments are not received until the beginning of the next month. This often occurs with credit card payments. Even though the credit card payment was accepted on the day of the treatment, the merchant deposit will likely be the month following, which creates a timing difference from month to month.

Lag is most noticeable when your collection percentage is very low at month's end (e.g. 80%) and then spikes the month following (e.g. 120%).

Treatment Conversion (Case Acceptance)

Another important KPI successful practices monitor and work to improve is how many clients move forward with additional treatments or services.

This element is the second piece of Jay Abraham's three ways to grow a business--increase average transaction value. The process starts with presenting a comprehensive treatment plan and concludes with the treatments being accepted.

Treatment conversion can be divided up into two categories:

a) High Value Procedures (HVPs) and
b) General dental procedures (GDPs)

HVPs include but are not limited to the following: Invisalign/ortho, multiple crowns/veneers in one visit, sleep appliances, periodontal surgery and implants.

It is important to recognize your conversion on HVPs will be lower than GDPs. The question is, what is a good treatment conversion rate for which to aim in each category? It is commonly stated that 1/3 of patients will always say yes, 1/3 will always say no and 1/3 are on the fence. It's the group who is on the fence who may choose to say yes or no, depending on how you present the treatment. Based on this logic, your treatment acceptance may range from 33-66%. Others state the average treatment acceptance rate in North America is 25% or less.

In my offices, the targets are as follows: HVPs are 50% and GDPs are 75%. I have found conversion on Invisalign is higher than on 3-3 veneers or 5 posterior crowns in one sitting. In addition, conversion on fillings and extractions is higher than on root canals. The goal is to have the average be at or above the targets listed above.

Take this with a grain of salt. You could argue that the average is a little higher or the peak is a little lower. There is no need to split hairs here, because the bottom line is that the trend is the message. The numbers simply tell a story about where to begin investigating. The numbers may mean you are under-planning on complex treatments, or you are simply not converting.

For example, if one of our doctors has an ultra-high conversion on GDP treatment plans it may be that they are simply under-diagnosing. Let me explain. If a doctor only diagnoses one-to-two fillings on a patient and has a treatment plan average of $400/patient, their conversion may approach 100%, whereas a doctor who has a comprehensive treatment plan of $3500/patient may be closer to 50 or 60%. Who is further ahead? On the other hand, if your conversion rate is very low (under 25%), you are clearly not converting.

The numbers simply direct you to where you should start looking so you can identify the root cause of the problem and begin to implement strategic solutions. You may be thinking, *I don't want to track all this--who has the time.* Well, that is entirely up to you. If you would rather stick with just one number then aim for 50% or higher as a treatment acceptance target for all procedures combined. Tracking this alone will be more than the majority of our colleagues are doing.

I have always wondered why the top 5% of practices were performing so much higher than most of the other offices. What I have found after much research and interviewing is that the top practices were far better at building nurturing relationships based on trust.

In his book *Outliers*, Malcom Gladwell explains that it takes approximately 10,000 hours of practice to achieve mastery in any field. I worked hard and became a good at being a dentist. I also became good at bringing in new patients because of the lessons I'd learned. But I was spending a ton of time with new patients, never to see them return.

What good is bringing in a ton of new patients if I couldn't get them to commit to treatment plans? That's when I had to move way out of my comfort zone and seek help. I discovered those practices which were achieving the highest treatment acceptance rates were winning by building trust and focusing on the relationship versus treating patients like a case number and bombarding them will technical jargon. There is a very simple science to this.

Low treatment acceptance is an indication that we're not building the relationship. We disguise that shortfall using excuses like:

- They just don't have the money
- My assistant didn't explain it right
- They don't value dentistry
- It's someone else's fault

The truth is, those excuses are just indications that we have not built a high-trust relationship with our clients. We need to look at ourselves and admit we're not winning in relationships, which means we're not winning in building trust, establishing communication or creating value and positive experiences.

Treatment acceptance, then, starts long before the treatment is even offered. The progression of the relationship is directly related to how your client feels throughout the process. How they feel begins with the very first phone call with your client. It continues with how they're received in your office. Your office should be clean and welcoming. The team should be friendly and helpful. The way your client is escorted into the treatment room and how they feel while they're in there waiting also counts. The experience carries all the way through the re-booking process and their departure, and it does not end there. The final step is the aftercare and follow-up. Then the process starts all over again. The more consistent the experience they have, the better the relationship will be, and therefore the more trust is created.

One of the best tactics I have implemented that made the biggest difference in my practice was going out into the waiting room to say hi to my patient before our appointment. I don't want the first time they see me to be in a treatment room. If they don't have one from our fridge already, I offer them a beverage. If time permits, I engage them in a short conversation. My warm smile and extra effort goes a long way.

I am going to challenge you to brainstorm with your team about what you can do in your practice to improve the relationship with your clients. You will come up with hundreds of ideas. Some of them will be simple and easy to implement, like what you say to a client when they arrive and how you say it. Some will require more time and investment. Some may seem small and trivial. Either way, make a list of ALL the problems and then test, test, test.

Learning Lesson

The easiest way to learn what your clients would like to see in your practice is to ask them. Customer surveys are valuable tools which give you direct feedback from the people who matter most—your clients.

Average Treatment Plan Value

More on Jay Abraham's second tenet of how to grow a business is increase the transaction average. One means to measure that is the average cost of a treatment plan (or average treatment plan value).

"Our study concludes that this is the percentage of our customers who will buy from us without any effort whatsoever on our part."

Look at your average treatment plan. When a new patient comes in, what's the average you diagnose right then and there?

Here's how to do it. Take a sum of all your treatment billings for new patients in a month and divide that by your total number of new patients. That is your *average cost of treatment plan.*

Monthly Sum of Treatments ($) / Total New Patients = Treatment Plan Average

The importance of this figure is to gauge the extent to which comprehensive treatment planning is taking place. I found most of the dentists in my practices should be averaging between $2000-2500 per treatment plan. We know that if we are open, honest and transparent with our recommendations, some clients will need $10,000 treatments and some may need $200, which would average to these figures above. Of course, your figures may vary depending on your fees, services offered, patient demographics, etc.

If doctors are averaging less than that, it is highly likely they are under-diagnosing. Some of the reasons for that include:

May lack confidence to present the treatment plan they feel is appropriate
Have a fear of rejection or push-back when the treatment plan is presented
Need additional education about alternative or complex treatments

Whatever the reason may be, we are not doing our clients any favors by under-diagnosing. I consider this a disservice to the patient and ourselves. We have a professional obligation to present the RIGHT treatment plan and explain the need for it in terms the patient can understand. Why else would we show up to work each day? There is something to be said about how phasing or the absence of phasing decreases treatment acceptance. A tendency to present too much information at one time or a large treatment can reduce case acceptance. That said, we should still be educating patients and presenting the necessary options, regardless of our fear of rejection or whatever else holds us back.

At first this may feel uncomfortable for you, but after a while it will become easier.

Here is another way to look at it. You're putting your patient, the client, in the position to make the best decision for themselves. That's it. If you fear presenting the right treatment plan and choose not to, you are essentially making the decision for your patient. This is an opportunity for you to step out of your comfort zone and reserve your judgment. This alone will make you millions over your career.

How would you feel if your mortgage broker decided which mortgage you should have? Or how about if your real estate agent decided which house you should buy? That is exactly what you are doing when you don't present the best treatment plan for your client. I often did this in the past, but seldom now, although I still slip up from time to time. I may judge someone and assume they don't want the treatment or may confuse introversion or anxiety with lack of interest. Whatever the reason, I now try to do my best to ensure every patient understands their problems, the consequences of going without treatment and the best solutions.

TIP: Track your total treatment diagnosed over a period of time and ensure it is 3x your production goal for that same period of time (example: daily, weekly, or monthly). For example, if you want to produce 5K per day you must aim to diagnose 15K per day. This assumes most dental offices will only convert 1/3 or less of their treatment plans.

Productivity

Back to Jay Abraham's tenets about the three ways to grow a business. Calculating your billing per doctor and hygienist is a great measure of efficiency and is an overall indicator of all three of the tenets. There are two ways to look at this:

~Billing-per-Hour (BPH)
~Overall Billings

Billings-per-Hour are a good efficiency indicator. Let's use the example of a four-operatory office whose office hours are eight hours-per-day, six days-per-week. The total available hours, otherwise known as capacity, is 32 hours per day or 192 hours per week. We can also take out lunches, downtime/turnover time per day for when the operatories are unavailable for setup and change over. For demonstration purposes, however, let's use 32 hours of usable chairs in the day.

When you take the total of your billings-per-day divided by your time in service, you will have your average billings-per-hour. Let's use this example with some figures.

You just finished up Monday and find your total services hours were 25 out of the 32 available. The recorded billings for the day were $18,000, so you calculate $720 BPH ($18,000/25). However, there were seven hours of available time not used. The net adjusted billing-per-hour is $562.50 ($18,000/32).

Now that you have a good handle on the logic, take a moment to think about how to dig a little deeper so you can get more visibility on your operations in the chair (whew...that was a lot of buzzwords). I use reports that calculate the BPH by doctor chair and by hygiene chair separately. This makes sense, doesn't it? You measure the performance of each differently, which means you can discuss how these goals can be used to schedule production. That is pretty cool. In the words of Jay Abraham, optimize, then maximize!

Both figures are valuable. The average billing-per-hour of $720 will tell you whether you are improving your efficiency of treatment delivery and increasing the size of treatment plans (Example: delivery of high value procedures or HVP) as compared to your history. The $562.50 average billing-per-hour will tell you the same, as well as your progress in managing capacity. An increase in BPH can indicate that your team is improving conversion, becoming more efficient or increasing the size of treatment plans, among others. The flipside is true in that a low or falling BPH is a symptom of a bigger problem.

The overall billings also provide a useful benchmark. You want the average billing in that dental chair to be about 25-33% production coming from the hygienists every month and about 67-75% production from the doctors. Keep in mind, there are tremendous costs associated with this, and it sounds great until you dissect it all down. Your practice needs to produce this to run a successful and profitable business.

Break Even Point (BEP)

One piece of low hanging fruit I think most practitioners are missing is the use of a daily Break-Even Point. In fact, I think many are oblivious to the use of a Break-Even Point (BEP) at all. Let's briefly discuss what a BEP is and then I'll explain how you can use it.

The Break-Even Point is exactly what it sounds like--the point at which your revenue is equal to your expenses.

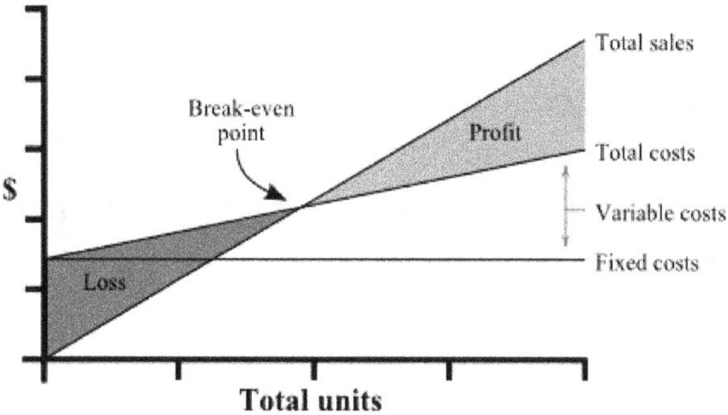

Even when used monthly, Break-Even provides a ton of usability. Remember earlier when I mentioned that a business cannot survive for long without cash flow? Break-Even is the number EVERY business must achieve to survive.

BEP can also be influenced by managing expenses. When a practitioner finds more efficient use of funds, can buy in bulk or otherwise can effectively reduce expenses, the BEP will drop. In other words, reducing your overhead either through fixed or variable expenses will reduce your Break-Even Point.

The biggest issue I see in so many struggling practices is that the Break-Even is only something used in a business plan, or at best, on an annual basis. I have had tremendous success by using the BEP daily.

This will involve using your Profit and Loss statement (P&L). Take it for a month, and then a quarter, and then over the course of the year in order to gather your data. Ideally, you want a full year of data.

Then ask yourself two questions:
Is this data accurate for the last year?
Have I added team members, has my rent increased or have any of my other expenses changed?

Once you have answered *yes* to the first question and you trust your data then you can work with the second question.

Normalize your P&L for those new expenses so you have an accurate depiction of your annual expenses and calculate the number of days you're going to be in the chair working. Exclude all Christmas holidays, long weekends, continuing education courses, birthdays, all other holidays, etc.

(Note: Take out expenses that are not actually true business expenses. Things like your car, housekeeper and anything else you are trying to put through your business that is actually a personal expense.)
Take your total expenses, both fixed and variable expenses (include your compensation and debt servicing requirements) and divide by the total working days you just calculated. That is your true daily overhead. Coincidentally, that is also your daily break-even point. You can extrapolate your monthly break-even point by multiplying this out by total number of days you are working that particular month.

That's the number you need to bill every day for you to break even. Anything over that number is profit. When you put this into practice, you should have a couple of revelations. You will realize that the daily number seems much more attainable than the annual number. You may also start to recognize how few profitable days your business has.

This simplistic method of calculation applies to most one-provider offices. Complexity in calculation arises with increasing providers and during growth phases of the office. Nonetheless, it can be calculated either way with a little more work.

An alternative method is to calculate your monthly break-even point as follows:

Monthly Over-Head (as per P/Ls) + Associate Pay(quarterly or semi-annual average) + Debt Service Payments + Your Compensation as an Owner (set monthly withdrawal if applicable or add yourself to the associate pay component if you pay yourself in the same manner your associates are paid) = Monthly Break Even Point.

NOTE: Including your compensation and debt servicing requirements is important. Why? Because your business must earn enough money to actually cover these expenses.

You (or better yet, your office manager or accountant/bookkeeper) should recalculate these figures periodically--monthly, quarterly or annually, whatever interval is right for your business. How often you redraft this report will depend on how often your expenses change, such as when you hire new staff, increase wages or buy/lease new equipment. This is a judgment call on your part. If your overhead doesn't fluctuate very much, there is no need to waste time (and money) with unwarranted reporting.

As your practice gets busier, there is little need or benefit from worrying excessively about using a few more consumables (if you have a system in place for RDA's in reference to operatory setup, sundries budgets and usage). This level of nitpicking will only cost you unnecessary time and expense to tell you what you already know. The goal is to know your BEP and exceed your daily/monthly/quarterly revenue.

If you are not a solo practitioner and don't work in the office, I recommend you choose to include your doctors' wages in your overhead. In our office, we calculate it both ways. Our target overhead excluding doctors' wages is 45-50%. Total profit after all doctors are paid 20-30% (depending on region, with the more common being 20%).

Now you have minimum target. You're not reading this just so you can earn the bare minimum. Let me ask you--how much do you want to earn? You know how much you need so you don't go broke. What figure will allow you to live the lifestyle you envision for yourself?

Re-Appointment

Getting your clients to rebook is perfectly in line with Jay Abraham's third tenet--increasing average transaction frequency.

At this point, you have provided your clients their first level of service and spent a lot of time and effort making them feel comfortable and building that trust relationship.

So now it is up to the client to come back when they feel the need to, right? I apologize for being a little facetious, but that is how most practices handle their business. The lifetime value of a patient drops dramatically when follow-up appointments are not rebooked. Depending on your cost of acquisition and treatment average (details about attracting and closing new clients are covered in the next chapter), that first visit may not be profitable for your practice.

A colleague of mine used to work for Daimler-Chrysler. He shared some interesting statistics with me. He said that the average client acquisition cost to attract a new customer was approximately $2800, while the cost to get a customer to re-purchase was only $800. The reason it was so much less to KEEP a customer than to attract a new one was because current customers already know, like and trust you.

How much effort do you think it is to ALWAYS be working with new patients? Getting to know someone and building a relationship takes a lot of energy at the start. It requires financial and emotional commitment. As the relationship builds, it becomes easier and feels more fulfilling. When your process fails to rebook your clients, you are throwing all that away to start over with someone else.

Now, if you're only interest is to get as many patients in through the door, sell them the most you possibly can in the moment and then move on to the next, then this book probably isn't for you.

If you're the type of doctor or practitioner who wants to provide a valued service to people and help them in a way very few people are qualified to do, please keep reading.

The measure we use in my practices is a benchmark of 85-95% or higher. For every 20 patients we see, 17-19 will rebook their next hygiene appointment. When the numbers start to dip below our benchmark, I know something needs to be addressed.

Here is an interesting dilemma. As the title of the chapter suggests, you can't manage what you can't measure. You need to start measuring how many patients rebook. You can do so in a variety of ways, depending on the size of your practice. We use a software program to do so, as well as manual calculations for data the software cannot produce. The software can calculate billings, patient reappointments, collections, new patient numbers and treatment conversions, among other things.

There are a few software tools you can use to track your clients through their customer journeys. A quick Google search will lead you to them. The important note here, in whatever means you choose, is that you are *measuring* your business so you can *manage* your business.

The metrics only point out that there may be a problem and help us narrow down where we need to look for solutions. There are a lot of moving parts in the operation of a dental office. Therefore, we are much better off knowing where to spend our time to correct uncovered issues instead of wondering why our business isn't growing or generating as much profit as we should.

The more important question to be answered is why your clients are not rebooking. There is no magic wand to figure this out. Sometimes the patient will tell you while in the chair. They may mention that they can't afford the treatment or that their insurance is maxed out. Sometimes they don't tell you, but they'll mention something to the hygienist or the receptionist on the way out. Many times, they don't tell you at all.

In every situation, once you know there is an issue, you can find ways to remedy the problem. If the issue is affordability or insurance, you can offer a payment plan. If the issue is comfort zone, you can educate the client and provide additional information or support. If the issue is dissatisfaction, you can address it right away instead of waiting for the client to stew over the issue or disappear completely.

A lot of people are afraid to tell us what's not good. They feel bad about mentioning the negative, but we encourage them to share because otherwise we can't improve. We've found many of our clients feel better about sharing their thoughts in a customer survey.

After all, the first step to fixing a problem is to know one exists.

There is another major benefit to tracking the reappointment percentage, and it isn't just about maximizing revenue opportunities. You can also use this measure to monitor performance of your doctors and hygienists.

Your reappointment percentage is more a measure of how well you and your team build high trust relationships. When you use the right tools, you can track this metric by doctor and hygienist. This may serve as an indication that more training is needed. Suppose one of your team members has an unusually low rebooking percentage. It is possible that he or she was just having an off month. If, however, he/she consistently has low numbers, he/she may need some help in how to build a better relationship with your clients and provide a high-value experience. The final alternative is that he/she is not a good fit for your culture and may need to be replaced.

These are some effective ways to use the metrics/KPI's to manage your practice. *You can't manage what you can't measure* has never been truer. The length of every line is perfect if you don't measure it.

Ideas to Remember

- Three ways for a business to profit are: sell more, spend less or both.
- How much you keep matters more than how much you make.
- Low collection percentage is an indication that cash is leaking out of your practice.
- Treatment acceptance is an indicator of how good you and your team are at building strong relationships with your clients.
- Put your client in a position to make the best decision for themselves.
- Billings-Per-Hour (BPH) should be measured on a per-doctor and per-hygienist basis to track efficiency and productivity.
- Use your daily Break-Even Point (BEP) as your daily minimum. Reverse engineer your daily production goals based on this number. (You will need to decide what your desired profit is prior to doing this calculation.)
- Reappointment percentage is another indicator of how good you and your team are at nurturing trust relationships with your clients.

CHAPTER FOUR

ROI-Based Marketing

"Half the money
I spend on advertising is wasted;
the trouble is, I don't know which half."
~John Wanamaker

Ask 1000 marketers about what you should do to grow your practice and you will get 2000 answers. I know, I even laughed a little while writing it, but it is so true! The point is that everyone has an opinion about how you should market your business, but then most of them will change their opinions. You will literally get 2000 answers from 1000 people.

Each of them brings forward their marketing toolbox and starts throwing around terms like SEO, SEM, AdWords, branding, mobile, web, funnels, landing pages, social media and so on--all of which feel extremely elusive for even the savviest practitioner. *But they're the experts* you think to yourself, *and they must know what they're doing.*

It is incredibly frustrating when they sell you hard, you pay them a boatload and there are little-to-no results.

***

Since I was operating with an entrepreneurial mindset, I naturally started to seek out advice from successful entrepreneurs in many different industries. I spoke to, met with and read about entrepreneurs who ran real estate businesses, oil and gas businesses, on-line businesses, media companies and of course, dental practices. I have easily spent over $1 million in my entrepreneurial education by attending conferences and mastermind groups. I also invested in personal coaching and mentorship AND will continue to do so for a lifetime. One of the first lessons I learned was the importance of lead generation.

Lead generation didn't seem quite as important to me when I first started out as a dentist. We all know we need to attract new patients to grow our practice, but it never really sank in until I also thought about those patients as clients. Businesses and entrepreneurs invest heavily into lead generation for their businesses. That's when the light bulb came on for me. If I invested in lead generation intelligently, like other successful business owners and entrepreneurs did, applying the strategies from these mentors and tweaking them to fit my purposes, I would be able to help more people, grow my practices.

Philosophy on Lead Generation

Here is a concept I learned through coaches and mentors that I want you to understand to help you with lead generation. It will help you to understand what the TRUE value of a lead really is. Once you understand the value of a lead, you will be able to implement ROI-based marketing in your dental business.

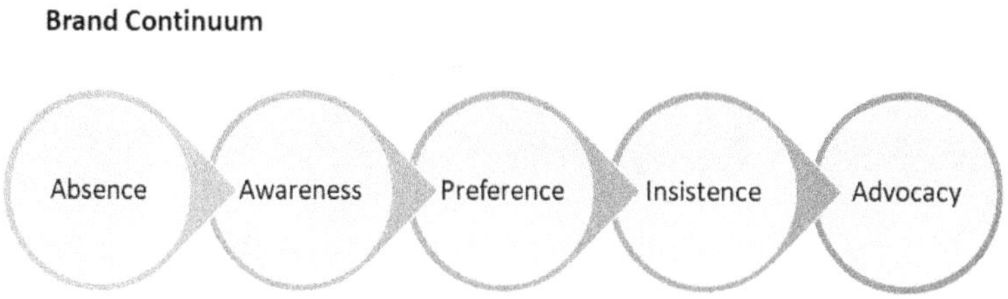

Brand Continuum

Absence → Awareness → Preference → Insistence → Advocacy

The brand continuum is an illustration of the different levels of branding for a business. I use this tool among others to gauge how well my marketing efforts are working. First, here's a brief explanation:

Absence	Brand absence means you have no brand. People have not heard about your business and awareness is practically non-existent. At this stage, you may be just starting up or are opening a new location.

	If no one knows about you or your dental business, they have no idea you could even be an option for them. Summary: You do not attract new patients or clients at this stage. You have not done any marketing.
Aware-ness	Brand awareness means prospective clients know about you and your business. They have a surface-level knowledge of your existence and can at least include you in their list of options. Awareness does not necessarily mean a purchase decision, though this is the first step. For example, a person can be aware that the Apple iPhone is an option but doesn't mean they will purchase an iPhone. The trap for most is that they invest marketing dollars into awareness but little in other strategies. Summary: You are marketing via direct mail, have a website and perhaps a social media presence. Potential new patients are looking at your ads but have not called your office or decided to attend.
Preference	Brand preference is when a client chooses your brand (product or service) over and above all of their other viable options but

	will gladly go somewhere else if your service is unavailable for some reason. Summary: The patient has decided to use your services but may chose to leave if another office offers more convenience or other features. Preference usually shows up as clients who choose another practice because of more convenient appointment times, better prices or incentives or newer technologies. This is the category most dental offices live in, with the majority of their patient base willing to jump ship due to preference. To shift from here to the next two levels, you must work on the patient retention strategies which will be discussed later in the book.
Insistence	Brand insistence is evident when a client will ONLY choose your service and nothing else, even to the point of extreme inconvenience or expense. Summary: These are your loyal patients who are not looking elsewhere. They are unlikely to jump ship due to a special offer, slightly lower pricing or some other convenience feature offered by your competitor. These are patients who have had one or more encounters with you and are impressed with their experience. You have

	WOWED them, and they TRUST you. They can be easily motivated to refer you patients and tell their friends about you, which allows them to progress to the next level.
Advocacy	Brand advocacy is the Holy Grail for a business and includes clients who not only insist on your services, they also tell everyone they know to use your service. Summary: These are your raving fans. Typically, they will have started in the brand preference category but due to multiple positive treatment outcomes, development and from nurturing the doctor/team/client relationship and numerous WOW experiences, you have generated a FAN! Consistency is the key to obtain a patient base like this. Your goal should be to move as many patients into this category as possible. If you can get 50% of your patients generating internal referrals for you, you are well on your way to creating and maintain a thriving practice.

Your question at this point is probably, "So what?" How does this link up with lead generation and ultimately getting me more clients?

When you look at each stage in this continuum from the perspective of a potential client, you will quickly realize your job as a business owner is to implement internal and external marketing and client retention strategies to move your clients from *Absence* through to *Advocacy*. Can you see how powerful that would be? The top 1% of practices and small business do a great job of getting as many patients as possible from brand awareness to brand advocacy. The simplest way to do that is get them in the door, develop a relationship, treat them like gold and do it consistently! We will cover more about client retention strategies that will allow you to move more patients into brand advocacy in Chapter Nine.

Lead generation is more than just putting an advertisement in your local paper or magazine. Lead generation is about making a connection with people who need dental services, want you to provide that service, will choose no one else but you and then tell everyone they know that you should also be their first choice. This is a process that starts with intelligently designed external marketing campaigns targeting specific patients, converting them into new patients when they call the office, delivering so much value that they feel you wowed them and then doing it consistently over the long-term. Consistency breeds trust, loyalty and ultimately, raving fans!

I hope that gets you excited. If you can't get fired up about your dental business, then why are you doing it?

One of the best places to start is at the beginning. Let's talk about the low-hanging fruit.

Building Awareness

Since I just mentioned that building awareness on its own is not very valuable, let's discuss briefly how to build awareness that *is* worth something. The goal is to curate a list of qualified leads whom you hope to attract as clients.

In the back of the book, I have included a list of 57 Lead-Generation Strategies you can use to build awareness and add to your list of qualified leads. As your marketing strategist will gladly point out, there are infinitely more strategies than the ones outlined. The point is, the only limit to lead-generation strategies is your imagination and your budget.

Executing this step alone is not going to get you where you want to go. If you were able to get 100 new leads but couldn't convert them, you'd have wasted your marketing dollars. If you converted 80% of your leads but couldn't keep them, you'd have wasted marketing dollars. As our friend John Wanamaker asks about wasting 50% of his advertising, *how do you know where and how to invest your marketing budget effectively*? Far too often, I hear dentists say, "I need more new patients." This may be true, but before I can determine that, I ask them how many NEW patients they get per month? How many leads do they generate (phone calls from prospects)? How many of the phone calls does your front desk convert? Finally, what is your case-conversion rate once you have a new patient in your chair? Most dentists I'm acquainted with don't know this information.

My answer to their question is, let's find out these answers and then we can determine if you have a lead-generation problem, a call-conversion problem or a case-conversion problem. Whatever the case might be, we can fix it, but we need to know what the problem is before we start throwing more money at marketing and lead generation.

******WARNING******

Lead Generation progressing through the brand continuum will require an investment in marketing.

When I finished dental school, I searched and interviewed at over 100 practices before I chose my first and only associate position. I worked for about two-and-a-half years in that practice. Through the early part of my career, I worked for a dentist who was 100% committed to marketing. Looking back, I would say that was the impetus for the philosophy I eventually adapted to build my practices.

At one point, I met a multi-practice doctor who suggested partnering. Eventually I invested in another office and grew to 52 team members across nine different offices. I am currently growing four start-ups, actively managing six dental practices and on the hunt for more acquisitions today.

Over that time, I learned a lot of lessons....

- The pain and discomfort of an empty chair
- The challenge of making payroll month after month
- What a bad partnership looks like
- How to choose the right office
- The process of litigation
- How to deal with failures
- The value of coaches and mentors

~The biggest and most important lesson I learned is to invest in marketing. You are one of three types of people:

A.) Those intrigued about how investing in marketing can make you money and grow your business.
B.) Those who roll their eyes and feel marketing is just an expense line and good dentists don't need to market their practice, or that marketing is somehow unethical.
C.) Those who market very little and still experience high new-patient numbers

If you are person A, you are well on your way. I am excited for you and what lies ahead for your business. You are several steps ahead of most people.

If you are person B, you are going to learn your lessons the hard way unless you shift your mindset. The good news is, you're just in time.
If you are person C, perhaps your practice is in a favorable dentist-to-patient population ratio which exhibits

favorable population demographics with most residents having insurance. Or maybe you are just that good at internal marketing. Whatever the reason, this is not everyone's reality. It is still important to educate yourself early and often to prepare for less-favorable times you may experience in the future.

Regardless of the category you are in, continue reading and I will show you exactly how I've invested in marketing to successfully grow my dental business.

I mentioned in the previous chapter that there are only three ways to grow your business. While the last chapter focused on increasing average transaction value and increase average transaction frequency, this chapter will focus on the other means to grow your practice--awareness and attracting new patients.

Learning Lesson

Sales is not a dirty word. You are going to have to shift your mindset around sales. The sale is more about something you do with someone than you do to someone. At its purest, sales is simply putting a person in the position to decide in their best interest.

This is what we do every day—give people all the information they need to make a good decision for themselves.

DISCLAIMER: FROM THIS POINT ON THERE WILL BE SAMPLE CALCULATIONS AND NUMBERS. IT'S A LOT FOR MOST PEOPLE BUT PLEASE FOLLOW THROUGH IT WITH ME SO YOU CAN GAIN AN APPRECIATION FOR THE FOLLOWING:

- How costly a mistake it is for you not to track your marketing ROI.
- The importance of implementing client retention strategies.
- Creating WOW experiences to convert new patients into raving fans.

Allow me to demonstrate....

Let's pretend you have a business that does the following:

- Has 100 clients
- Each client pays $100 every time they buy
- Each client buys 10 times per year

The annual revenue of this business is $100,000 (100 clients x $100 purchase x 10 purchases). To increase the total revenue by 10% to $110,000, all you need to do is either to get 10 more clients, get your current clients to spend $110 per transaction or get them to buy 11 times. That is a 10% increase in any one of those areas. You could easily increase your business by 10% by marketing more effectively.

Now, how about 30%? Do you think you could increase your business by 30% just as easily? To do that, you would have to get 30 new clients, get your current clients to spend $30 more per transaction or get them to buy 13 times per year. That's a tougher one to manage, but I know it's possible, because I've done it. Simply compound your marketing efforts to increase each area by 10% at the same time!

Look...

110 clients x $110 purchase x 11 purchases = $133,100 or ~ +33% increase!

How do you get a 30% year-over-year increase in revenue for your dental practice? By increasing marketing and internal referrals to generate new clients. Comprehensive treatment planning and acceptance will increase the average transaction value (case conversion), while an effective hygiene department can increase your transaction frequency (reappointment). The message here is to invest in marketing.

Full Circle

All of your marketing investment must be focused on one or a combination of these three purposes. Your marketing efforts must be focused on either gaining new clients, bringing in a higher transaction value or higher transaction frequency or all the above. Your challenge is going to be which one to focus on and when.

"What gets measured gets improved."
~Peter Drucker

I love this statement by legendary management consultant Peter Drucker. I guess why I enjoy it so much is because I have felt the pain of getting it wrong. I have been that entrepreneur who invested dollar after dollar without knowing if I was getting a return from it.

The message here is you need to track EVERYTHING. That may seem obvious to you here and now, but you would be surprised how much cash flow is leaking out of your business. The worst part is, most doctors don't even know how much money is being lost or how many blown opportunities they have had. I follow Peter Drucker's advice to measure and improve everything I can.

When I started, I found out that I was getting lost in the details and didn't really know what to do with the numbers. Eventually, I learned to start simple and stick to the basics. I would like you to learn from my mistakes. One of my favorite lines that my wife shared with me is, *a wise person learns from their mistakes while a genius learns from the mistakes of others*. I know you are a genius and can learn from my mistakes.

Let's start off with the basics and keep it simple. You need to know some basic measurements to implement effective ROI-based marketing.

ROI (TRUE ROI) - Return on Investment - The net amount of profit divided by the cost of your investment times 100 (Profit/Cost x 100). This is expressed as a percentage (%).

ROA - Return on Activity - The gross revenue generated minus the applicable gross marketing expenses, divided by the applicable gross marketing expenses times 100 (Revenue-gross marketing expenses/gross marketing expenses x100). This is expressed as a percentage (%).

NOTE: Both ROI and ROA require you to calculate either the net profit or the revenue directly generated from a particular marketing campaign. This is time-consuming and cumbersome to complete and may not be worth the effort. Instead, we use a Simplified ROA/ROI calculation which will be easy to calculate and will give you the information you require to determine those marketing campaigns which are working and those which are not.

Simplified ROA/ROI: The average revenue generated by the campaign divided by the applicable gross-marketing expenses times 100 (Average Revenue/Related marketing expenses x 100) ***The key difference here is the manner in which average revenue is calculated. This will be described in a box later in this chapter.

Revenue Per New Patient - The total adjusted revenue for your office over a 12-month period (or period of time) divided by the total number of new patients over that same time period times 100 (Total revenue 12 months/Total NP's same 12 months x 100)

LTV - Lifetime Value - The lifetime value of a customer and the total amount of revenue a client brings over the length of the relationship. Revenue Per New Patient X Period of retention (a 5, 10, 15, or 20-year period, depending on how confident you are that you retain your patients for the period of time chosen). For demonstration and simplicity, we'll assume Revenue Per New Patient is $2000 and the retention period is five years.

CPL - Cost Per Lead - The average cost to generate a qualified lead or what it costs to generate a phone call.

CAC - Client Acquisition Cost - The average investment required to attract each new client. In other words, this is what it costs to get a patient in the chair. The difference between CPL and CAC is predominantly influenced by your call-conversion rate.

Here's an example of how these measurements are used. Assume you spent $50,000 in advertising last year which generated 166 new qualified leads and you closed 50 new clients for your dental business. For each client you have, assume the average client stays with you for approximately five years and spends an average of $2000 per year in treatment plans and maintenance.

These are the numbers you need to create a foundation for ROI-based marketing.

CPL = $301.20/lead ($50,000 ad spend/166 new leads)
CAC = $1000/client ($50,000 ad spend/50 new clients)
LTV = $10,000/client ($2000 client spend/year x 5 years)
ROA = 900% ([$10,000 LTV - $1000 CAC]/$1000 CAC)

Challenge Your Understanding

Suppose one of your newly acquired clients is so impressed with the quality of your service and their experience that they send you a referral. What is the ROA of that referral and how would that change the LTV of the happy client?

The ROA of the referral is priceless. Since the LTV of the referral of the new client is $10,000 in our example and it did not cost you anything to acquire the referral, the calculation is $10,000/0 and cannot be defined. On the other hand, the LTV of your happy client who provided you the referral just doubled to $20,000 and their ROA more than tripled to 1900% [($20,000 LTV-$1000 CAC]/$1,000 CAC).

In other words, a happy and loyal client who refers happy and loyal clients is worth a fortune to your business.

These figures are oversimplified and just used to illustrate the concept. One may argue that the lifetime value above is incorrect because most patients stay up to 20 years or most patients spend less than $500-$1000 in a year. In this case, the LTV would be between $10K-$20K per patient. The bottom line is that your patients are valuable and tracking these figures will drastically improve how you are able to manage your dental practice. Remember at the beginning of the chapter when I discussed John Wanamaker's quote about knowing which 50% of his advertising is being wasted?

Light bulbs should be going off for you right now. Take this concept back to the list of over 57 lead-generation strategies. With these three simple calculations, you will be able to compare the VALUE of each lead-generation strategy and continue investing only in the strategies with the highest ROI. Don't worry. You don't have to do this manually. You can place call-tracking numbers on most marketing pieces/modalities and software can track it for you.

This is such an important piece of what it takes to build a dental practice that serves your life instead of consuming your life, whatever that means for you. Does it mean making more money, having more time, less stress, creating a lucrative legacy or being able to give more to your charities or communities?

I had to learn this lesson the hard way and wish I'd had someone show me these concepts earlier in my career. I was at a point in my practice where I was feeling confident about what I was doing. I was anxious to attract more clients to my business and believed that the more I spent on advertising, the more clients I would get. The logic seemed sound at the time.

In reality, what I found was that as my ad spend increased, the number of new patients didn't increase. I had doubled my ad spend and only acquired on average of five new patients per month over the next 90 days! I was using a combination of print advertising and radio. Truthfully, I wasted a ton of money on advertising. I just wasn't putting my dollars to work in the highest ROI channel. I am not suggesting that print or radio advertising are poor strategies. The issue was that I had no basis of comparison until I implemented a system to measure how EFFECTIVE each strategy was performing.

The concept is simple but not necessarily easy. You're going to need to be patient, and believe me, your patience will be tested! Make sure to temper your expectations as you invest in your marketing efforts. Not every lead-generation strategy you implement will work. Some of them will need time and some will never work no matter what you do. The only way you will know is to test, test and test.

Be selective. This is not the time for you to take this knowledge and execute a spray-and-pray approach to your marketing. Before you choose which lead generation strategies to implement, speak to your current and past clients. Ask them where they went to find your practice. Find out what their preferences are and where they like to get their information. Do they default to Google search? Did they ask friends and family for recommendations? Did they see an ad and how did they respond?

Since you now know which measurements to track, including Simplified ROA/ROI and CAC, you will be able to optimize your strategies and generate the highest possible return for your marketing efforts. I have found that even direct mail can produce amazing results when the layout is well-designed, the offer is attractive, and it is delivered with the appropriate frequency. I would have never found out if I didn't track everything.

To this point, we have only scratched the surface of how you begin to track the ROI on your marketing and lead generation efforts.

Once you really start paying attention to the return you are getting on your marketing investments, you will start to notice a few trends. The most obvious trend will be what is working well and what isn't, which will lead you to two very important decisions:

In which marketing strategies do I continue to invest?
Which modalities do I need to STOP?

In my experience, answering the second question and deciding which marketing modalities I need to stop has saved me more trouble than I can express. When you consider any of the lead-generation strategies available to you, if you are seeing even a slightly positive return, an increase is still an increase. Warren Buffet said the first rule of investing is not to lose money. The same applies here. The more you can mitigate losing money when you are investing in marketing strategies, the sooner your gains will take over. Then you will increase in confidence in what you are doing.

Knowing when to STOP investing in marketing that has no ROI requires knowing your numbers and having patience.

Knowing your numbers

This ties back to our lengthy discussion about tracking everything. Let me give you a few situations to suggest how you can apply this: (For demonstration purposes, we'll use the ROI below using the estimated LTV of the patient. It is not important to focus on the exact numbers, but rather the information it provides and the questions it answers.)

You have been attending trade shows to get out and meet with prospective patients. You know you have invested $20,000, which includes the trade show booth for two days, print materials, prizes to give away, your time to attend the booth, set up, tear down and travel time for you and any staff you brought to help you. You have also been diligent about tracking everything, so you have your list of 20 people you spoke with at the event. You compare that list to your list of patients every month. After three months of follow-up, you find you only attracted one new client from that event. Since you know your numbers, you conclude...

Cost-Per-Lead = $1000 ($20,000 spend / 20 leads)
Client Acquisition Cost = $10,000 ($20,000 spend / 1 client)
Lifetime Value = $10,0000 (Est $10,000 x 1 new client)
ROA = -50% ([$10,000 LTV - $20,000 spend]/$20,000 spend)

Note: LTV is used to simplify this calculation and enhance your understanding. In reality, you may have acquired three leads that bought nothing at all, or three that did 30K treatment plans each.

You acquire a mailing list of 20,000 from a local marketing firm and schedule four quarterly mailings over the next year. The total cost of this lead strategy after you've hired a professional designer to design the mailer, paid for the print and postage and accounted for the time spent for your team to follow up on the inquiries and book the appointments is $21,000. Over the course of the year and for three months after you finish your campaign, you were able to get three new clients. As you review the numbers, you conclude:

Cost-Per-Lead = price paid for your list / 20,000 leads
Client Acquisition Cost = $7000 ($21,000 spend / 3 clients)
Lifetime Value = $30,000 (Est $10,000 per client x 3 new clients)
ROA (campaign) = +43% ([$30,000 LTV - $21,000 spend]/$21,000 spend)

You have decided to venture into promoting your practice online because you've heard some good things about search advertising. You hire a digital advertising agency to help you and test the waters. The agency charges you $10,000 for the entire campaign, which includes keyword research, ad spend (based on clickthrough), optimization, management and list building. At the end of the campaign, the agency provides you with a list of 10,000 people with whom to follow up. During your review of the numbers, you observe the following:

Cost-Per-Lead = $1.00 per lead ($10,000 spend / 10,000 leads)
Client Acquisition Cost = TBD - to break even, you would need one new client.
Lifetime Value = TBD
ROA (campaign) = TBD

Based on the information above, which method do you continue with and which do you stop? It appears Scenario A was a complete bust and you may never want to use that modality going forward. The Cost-Per-Lead is very high, and the ROI is negative. The results from Scenario B look promising. The Cost-Per-Lead is likely to be reasonable and the ROI is positive. The results for Scenario C are not complete yet so it would be difficult to make a permanent decision on that yet, though the Cost-Per-Lead is very low and the break-even in clients appears attainable.

Simply based on knowing your numbers, you would be able to conclude that the first method is a complete waste of marketing investment while the other two methods appear to be more worthwhile. This is a great start to keeping things simple. However, I am here to tell you the real world of running a business in your field of practice is not quite this simple, but you are now more prepared to start asking pointed questions about why one strategy appears to work so much better or worse than the others.

Here are some questions I would ask about each of these scenarios:

- Was the trade show in Scenario A the wrong show for the patients we need to attract? Was it the wrong type of audience?
- Was the team ineffective in our follow-up from the trade show?
- Did we follow up long enough after the trade show?
- Did we max out our return from the direct mailing? ~Would we have increased the return if we'd increased the frequency of mail outs?
- Could we have acquired a similar direct mailing list for less money?
- Was the agency effective in their bidding process? Are there other agencies who can provide leads for less?
- What is their agency fee vs. media spend? Are there other agencies who can provide leads for less?

Sit back and take a deep breath. There are many software tools and companies who do this work and can give you all the help you need to succeed. You do not need to be the expert on all of these strategies. I don't want you to be. Because if you are spending time becoming the point person on all of this, you're back to working IN your business. That is the opposite of what I want for you

Learning Lesson

After many rounds of strategy, texting and adjustment, I have found three dimensions to a successful mailer campaign:

~Tracking number and conversion goal.
~Irresistible call-to-action (CTA) to visit a landing page or download a lead magnet.
~Reengagement or retargeting strategy.

A tracking number and conversion goal can be as simple as a unique phone number or website URL used only in that campaign to track how much engagement your campaign generates.

The call-to-action is the instruction of what you want the potential client to do: "Call this number," or, "Visit this website," or, "Complimentary Service," such as whitening, electric toothbrush or exam.

Reengagement or retargeting are buzzwords which indicate how you use the potential client's action to get them in front of other marketing messages. There are a lot of really effective tools for retargeting in online marketing.

With any modality, I target a *MINIMUM* return of three-to-four times my spend. The figures we used above are illustrative only. You may find your results to be much different, but you will never know unless you are tracking everything and then know when to stop investing in marketing that has No ROI.

***

I promised you a deeper dive on some of the numbers in ROI-based marketing. We have already introduced a few of the concepts and I will give a little more background into each one.

Cost-Per-Lead

You'll find that most of these terms are self-explanatory. CPL is a number that means exactly what it says. How much did you spend to get a lead? How you define a lead is up to you. I prefer to work in terms of *qualified* leads, meaning the lead has a need AND a want for my services. Another way I like to look at this is that leads are phone calls which have not yet converted.

In my practice, a qualified lead is a person who has a want, need or desire for my dental services AND has a means to pay for them. The ability to pay is very important. Qualified leads either have the means to pay out of pocket, have insurance coverage or a combination of the two.

Learning Lesson

A business can survive for a period of time with no profit. It cannot survive without cashflow.

Profit is needed to grow your practice. The returns from positive marketing investments can be used to reinvest in other marketing initiatives. However, if the practice does not get paid for the work eventually, the lack of cashflow will choke the practice.

A practice can operate for a time with zero profits so long as there is enough cashflow to pay for the operations. Salaries can be paid, supplies can be purchased, and leases can be covered if there is enough cashflow from sales that are not necessarily profitable.

**Profit = EBITDA (earnings before interest, depreciation, taxes, amortization); operating profit*

Calculating the Cost-Per-Lead is simple.

Total Spend to Generate the Leads / # of Leads = Cost Per Lead ($)

This is metric is important for two purposes:

Comparing marketing strategies within a modality (e.g. Google AdWords vs. Facebook)
Back-engineering ROI

Cost-Per-Lead is useful when comparing strategies in the same modality. This is because not all leads are created equal. You may spend $1.50 per lead through an on-line source, or $350 per lead through something more interactive, like an event. The differences are between conversions. An individual you met in person at an event is much more likely to close than an online lead who opted into a mailing list.

That does not mean either one is more valuable than the other. It just means you can compare one event to the other when it comes to Cost-Per-Lead. Or you can compare Cost-Per-Lead between Google AdWords and Facebook when you execute online marketing.

The great equalizer across all modalities is Client Acquisition Cost.

Client Acquisition Cost (CAC)

Total Spend / # Clients Acquired = Client Acquisition Cost ($)

> *Note: A client is considered acquired when they book an appointment and/or show up for that appointment.*

This is another simple AND powerful tool to measure your results and direct your activity. It is also the great equalizer across all modalities. You have already seen a couple examples of this earlier when we discussed tracking everything. Truly, this metric is one to be closely watched.

Would you spend $15,000 to get a client whom you know is only going to bring you $10,000? Of course not. The CAC is useful in two different ways:

Comparing marketing strategies across different modalities (e.g. Google AdWords vs. Tradeshow)
Guideline for how much you could spend

The CAC is one of the few metrics that compares apples-to-apples when it comes to marketing methods. Consider the list of 57 lead-generation strategies. They all require different budgets and time to manage. The only way to compare them is to measure how much you need to spend to attract a client.

Let's look at our AdWords versus Trade show example.

	Google Adwords	Trade Show
Cost per lead	$1.50	$350
Marketing Investment	$10,000	$10,000
Total Leads	6667	28
Closing rate	1%	30%
# New Clients	66	8
Client Acquisition Cost	$151	$1250

When you compare the two modalities, it's clear in this illustration that the Google AdWords lead-generation strategy is far more valuable, because it generates new patients for almost 1/10 of the cost. These figures are just used to illustrate the point and your results will likely be much different.

I also said CAC is a guideline for how much you could spend. Using this knowledge, you can back-engineer how much you would need to spend to increase your patient list by 10%, 20% or 30% if you wanted to.

***** **IMPORTANT** *****

The Lifetime Value (LTV) of a patient is the highest amount you would be willing to spend to acquire that patient. Think about that for a moment. The most you would be willing to spend to get a new patient (CAC) is equal to the total amount that client is worth to you in your practice (LTV). This is why putting in a tracking system and knowing your numbers is so important. The more accurate you are in calculating LTV, the more efficient your marketing spend will be.

Does that make sense?

So, if the Lifetime Value of your patient is $10,000, then in theory, you should be willing to spend just a little less than $10,000 to acquire that patient. Hopefully you will be spending much, much less, but you get the point.

Return on Investment (ROI)

The entire focus of this chapter has been ROI-based marketing, and all the discussion has been leading up to this point. Calculating True ROI:

[Total Revenue Generated from a campaign - Total Spend = Total Profit] / Total Spend x 100 = Return on Investment for campaign (%)

As I mentioned earlier, calculating True ROI as described above is time-consuming and in many cases is not possible to do accurately. Given this, we'll focus on a modified version called Simplified ROA/ROI. Are your asking yourself why I didn't just cut to the chase? Reason: I want you to have the background information. An educated consumer is the best consumer. You are now equipped with the skills required to hold your marketing companies accountable and ensure you get the most for your hard-earned dollars. As well there are a number of companies that claim they track ROI when in reality they are tracking Simplified ROA/ROI. You can now ask the right questions because you understand the difference.

Important Note:

Calculating TRUE ROI can be painful and you could easily spend more time crunching the data than making use of the results. Below is a Simplified Method of Calculation:

Total revenue per new patient: Total revenue over period of time/Total new patients during that same time period

e.g. Annual revenue $1,500,000/600 new patients in that year = $2500 per patient
This is then used as the average new patient value when calculating ROI/ROA for a particular method.

Example:
$20K on a direct mail campaign resulted in 15 new patients.
$2500 per new patient x 15 new patients = $37,500

Simplified ROI/ROA = Average Total Revenue (Campaign)/Total Cost (Campaign)

Or

$37,500/$20,000 = 1.8x

This is a very simplified calculation which can provide some guidance and is commonly used in high-performance practices.

The calculation and the use are the same. The only thing that changes are the inputs. As your marketing efforts and business management become more sophisticated, you will be able to drill down deeper on the different methods.

What I found while growing my practices was that I wanted to get additional insights about where my clients were coming from and the correlation with which treatment plans they accepted. I started to build marketing systems to measure true ROI. The goal was to get to a point where I could track the exact amount of revenue I was generating for any given client and how much I spent to market and service that client.

This was incredibly useful but required a time commitment to track the numbers. In my opinion, it is valuable but not necessary. If you implement the simplified ROA/ROI you are way ahead of the game. I also want to note that not all marketing modalities can be tracked. Exactness and perfection are a significant challenge here.

There is a good chance a patient hears about you on the radio, finds you through a Google search, checks out your reviews, visits your website and finally calls the number on the top of your website to book an appointment. You have both a call-tracking number and internal measures (mandate the team to ask how the new patient heard about you) to ensure you know where the lead was generated. The call-tracking number states the website was the source, but the patient tells your team they found you on Google. The real source for the lead was the radio. This is a reality. The good news is, many lead generation strategies can be tracked exactly. It may be imperfect, but I can promise you, tracking and making every effort to stay on top of your numbers is going to save you hundreds of thousands of dollars over your career.

I encourage you to use call-tracking numbers and a company that can gather the following information for you:

- Determine the number of leads generated from a modality.
- Listen to the calls for quality assurance and ensure the front desk is converting the calls to new patients.
- Determine the Simplified ROA/ROI on your ad spend.
- Track how much you are spending as a percentage of your revenue.

Most business owners are not doing their own marketing or micromanaging their marketing campaigns. They don't have the knowledge, time or passion, and that is fine. That is why we have marketing companies. The issue is, marketing companies all talk a good game and take your money, yet only a few deliver great results. Here are a few tips to help you find a reputable company that can deliver results. (Warning: No guarantees. This just minimizes the risks.)

Ask the marketing company:

- If they specialize in dental marketing or to provide the number of dental clients they serve.
- What their client retention rate is.
- The number of years they have been in business.

- If you can speak to three of their clients who have been with them 12 months or more.
- The expectations regarding the number of generated leads and if they track this in-house.
- Do they require that you sign any contracts with them? (Contracts into which you are locked in for a certain period of time are red flags for me. I much prefer to work with companies that know they need to work hard to keep my business or the following month I am gone.)
- Do they use original content (SEO companies mainly here) and if so, what is the cost associated with copywriting?
- Online: Who owns the website and its content? You should own all the assets.
- Do they offer regional exclusivity to their clients or are they going to do marketing for the dental office down the street, as well?
- Can they provide you with samples, especially if using print ads? Compare those to others (your staff have received at their home addresses if they live in your target area). Is your offer the same? Will yours stand out in a mailbox next to your competitors'?

Ideas to Remember

- The Brand Continuum is the journey a client takes from absence to advocacy.
- There are only three ways to grow a business: Attract new clients, increase average transaction value per client or increase transaction frequency per client.
- Track everything, starting with the basics: Cost-Per-Lead (CPL), Client Acquisition Cost (CAC) and Simplified Return on Investment/Activity (ROI/ROA).
- Stop investing in marketing with no ROI/ROA.
- Continue testing and re-testing your marketing.

CHAPTER FIVE

Relationships, Relationships, Relationships

"When you're surrounded by people who share a passionate commitment around a common purpose, anything is possible."
~Howard Schultz

I agree *relationships* can be a buzzword, but I don't feel you can get anything accomplished unless you put an effort into forming relationships. One of the reasons the concept feels like a buzzword is relationships can be somewhat superficial. So many people say they want to build strong and meaningful relationships but do not act like it. Then there are relationships truly built on high trust and value. When you really connect with people, magic happens, and things get done.

This book is meant to take you on an entrepreneurial roller coaster with a mix of soft skills and solid tactics. Building relationships is neither a soft skill nor a solid tactic. They are a beautiful necessity.

Learning Lesson

What is the product of the product? The real reason people purchase anything is not for the item or service itself, but what it does for them. A car, a smartphone, a trip. A client will choose the service which best gives them the satisfaction of what it is they want. Does a patient come in to get a cleaning because they want to prevent gum disease or do they just like the way it feels?

Perhaps the immediate gratification is that the cleaning feels good afterward, but there is also the fear of negative consequences--tooth loss, systemic illness, bad breath or social stigma, etc. Patients are motivated by emotion—negative consequences of no treatment.

Clients are motivated by emotions and back up their decisions with logic. Figuring out the client's real motivation (positive or negative) for accepting a treatment is a thoughtful and genuine way to build trust. It is the foundation of a good relationship.

With respect to our patients (aka clients), we only get to see many of them once or twice per year. I feel that the importance of relationships, particularly in healthcare, is about taking a genuine interest in people. Treating patients as a case number sounds a little cliché, but it continues to happen. Patients are people and want to be treated like human beings. I understand the need to be objective and impartial, but there's also a need to be compassionate and understanding. We don't need to separate these responses. If you haven't had a patient who has come in with preconceptions about dentistry and maybe some baggage, then you haven't been a dentist for very long. Some patients have an acquired fear of being in a dentist's chair. On the other hand, some patients show up positive and upbeat. The goal must always be about building rapport with either type of patient.

You owe you patients that. They took the time to book an appointment and most likely had to take time from work to visit your office. Many don't want to be there and some outright despise it. They are often stressed out by being in the dentist's chair. But they showed up anyway. The least you can do is show them genuine interest. Some days can be hard. Patients can be tough. This is your opportunity to lead by example and be the good you want to see in the world. Show your team what it looks like to step up and elevate the culture.

It starts with a conversation--a conversation which leads to learning interesting facts about each other and finding similarities. Trust is built through sharing and genuine interest.

At the beginning of every appointment with a new patient, have a chat and get to know them. I find out about their family, if they have children, what they do for work and things they like to do in their off time. Here's a tip. I also share with them! My patients get a chance to get to know me, as well. I don't think any professional today can go anywhere or accomplish any level of significance without this.

Here's another tip. My assistant writes down what we learned about the patient in the chart, such as *loves basketball, just got a motorcycle* or *going to Hawaii this winter with family*. This leaves me with a point of reference and an ice breaker at our next visit. You'll never get tired of hearing, "Wow, Doc, how did you remember that about me?!" Even if they don't say it, and even if they know you took notes, they'll still appreciate the effort, and it helps them connect to us.

Very little can be accomplished by the practitioner who only takes the authority level and issues treatments as if they are orders. You know what I am talking about. The outdated version where the doctor is the authority, the client is the patient and that's it. I tell, and you do. I couldn't figure out why patients wouldn't accept my treatment plans or rebook their appointments. When I started my career, I expected that after I explained all the science and used the correct technical terms, clients would be wowed by my brilliance and convert. All that did for my clients was confuse them, and a confused mind doesn't buy.

It wasn't until I figured out the product of the product. Why were patients really coming into my office? It wasn't to have me work in their mouth, scraping their teeth and gums with dental tools. I needed to be the one who gave them what they wanted instead of trying to take from them what I wanted.

"You will get all you want in life,
if you help enough other people get what they want."
~Zig Ziglar

Whatever their reason for coming in that day, the one thing your patient wants is to have that part nurtured. They want painless, efficient dentistry that comes with longevity and does not break the bank. These are common traits among most clients. Most don't know much about dentistry. They rely on what they do know and how we make them feel about it. That's why it is so important to address the clients' concerns FIRST and then point out any other issues after that has been resolved. Otherwise, their concerns are all the patient can think about, even after you have mentioned that you will address them during the appointment.

Whether the solution requires veneers, fillings or perhaps a root canal, patients need to trust us when we explain the procedures, so they feel like they are getting the product of the product. It is your job to give them value through education so they can make an informed decision. That should sound familiar, as I mentioned it as part of the definition of sales.

> *Product of the Product*
> *The product of the product is what clients are actually buying. When a consumer buys a car, they are not buying the car for the assembly of metal and plastic parts. They are buying it for what the car will do. That may be reliable, safe transportation, image, convenience or income (such as a taxi or Uber).*
> *When your clients agree to your treatment plans, they are buying what the plan will do for them—alleviate pain, maintain healthy teeth, improve their self-esteem, etc.*

You have heard the line *we need to give before we get.* When in reality it is more along the lines of, we need to give and give and give before we get. I promise you that if you focus on building the relationship, you will begin to see the results in all other aspects of your business--treatment acceptance, new patient flow, re-appointment percentage, and so on.

If building a successful practice requires strong, high-value relationships and the foundation of those relationships is trust, how in the world do I build trust?

- Walk into the operatory or first patient encounter with your shoulders back, head up and a smile on your face. People decide whether they trust you within the first few seconds of seeing you. Doing this will greatly increase the chances that this patient will perceive you as a kind, confident and trustworthy person.
- Treat people well. (Be kind, non-judgmental, excited to see them and thank them for being there.)

- Let them get to know you. (Open up and tell them about yourself. Share stories about your family and your hobbies and discover common interests.)
- Get to know them. (Use the Dale Carnegie Conversation Stack if you need a place to start. I suggest not being so formal. Talk to them like a friend and take a genuine interest in them.)
- Don't be pushy. (Pushy feels like sales. The art of treatment presentation will be discussed briefly later in the book.)
- Deliver value through education (but be careful of TMI).
- Be consistent in your actions. (Consistency in the experience builds trust.)
- Communicate transparently and don't speak "over their heads" (technical jargon etc.).
- Don't forget about them after the transaction (do post-op calls).

With Respect to Clients

It may seem a little too obvious, and you may even be thinking *yes, I already know this, Dr. Justin.* Well that is fine, but I like to remember this Confucius quote: *"To know and not to do is not yet to know."* If you knew it, you would already be doing it.

When it comes to treating people well, it is as simple as treating them the way they want to be treated. Some clients prefer to be doted on or have their hand held, while others prefer a more direct approach. All clients deserve to be treated with respect. You would be surprised how condescending some other doctors can be. I am guilty of it myself some days, and no one is perfect. I don't claim to be. When I slip up, I make sure to recognize it, accept accountability, learn and move on. It's more important to make progress (not perfection) through small daily improvements which lead to exceptional results over time. Achieving 100% is not the goal, because that is unrealistic.

Let your clients get to know you. If your conversations with your client sounds like a job interview, with you asking rapid-fire questions and your clients trying to tell you the answers you want to hear, then you have work to do. People won't buy your skills or service. They buy why you're doing it. Tell them your story. You will be surprised by how interesting you are.

Get to know your patients. Enough said.

Being pushy is a funny trait among most doctors I meet. What they think is pushy really is not. What they don't think is pushy really is. Are you one of these doctors? There is an element of social intelligence here but let me add some clarity. Presenting a treatment plan with a solid explanation is not pushy. Asking for clarifications on objections is not pushy. Asking repeatedly to the point of making someone mistrust you is pushy. There is no secret trick here. If you're not sure, ask someone you trust if you're being pushy.

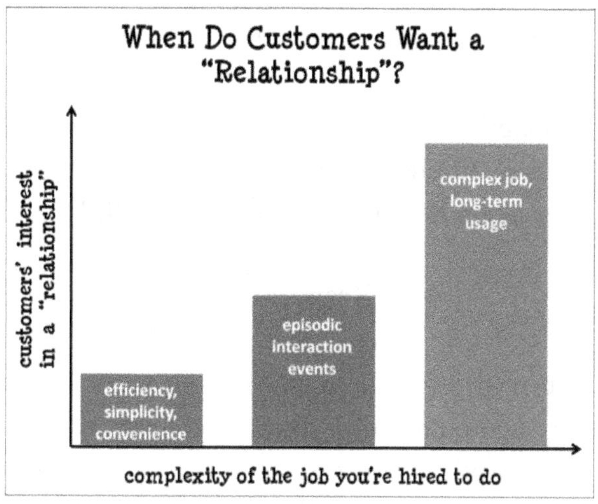

On the last point with respect to clients--what doctors feel is education and support may be intimidating for a patient. I train a lot of my staff in this area and observe that they are so proud of their knowledge level that they want to demonstrate their expertise and use industry jargon. They miss the point, which is client understanding. Instead of building trust, they effectively make withdrawals from the relationship bank account. Clearly, we work in a technical field and we have certain obligations. However, improving our skills to explain complicated or technical procedures using visuals, graphics and common language will put trust back into our client relationships. Pretend you are walking with them 'down the stairs of understanding,' where the bottom is the best decision patients can make for themselves.

In my office, we keep a binder full of images pertaining to different treatments. Not only before and after pictures, but also drawings and sketches of what the procedures look like. I keep it chairside, along with other patient education materials which allow me to explain to different procedures to different types of learners. (you can also use an iPad or tablet if you prefer something a little fancier)

With Respect to Team

Pay them well. Give them challenging tasks. Give them autonomy and authorship. Recognize them often and reward them well. These are some of the most valuable means to treat your team well.

Open up a little more with your team and break bread with them from time to time. You can let them get to know you as you would a friend. Invite them to meet your family. It's more than okay to socialize with your team. It's even an advantage. Include them in your dream-building and allow them to be part of your journey. You're a part of theirs.

You need to get to know your team. If you can't remember their names, you are in trouble. In addition to knowing their names make note of their birthdays and the names of their spouse and children. I know you are an over-achiever and you can get much deeper than that. Do you know their favorite lunchtime meal? Or how about their favorite restaurant? When you start to learn some of these traits you can surprise your team with some very welcome gifts and rewards.

With Respect to Vendors

Your vendor relationships can have a tremendous impact on your practice, good or bad. You may have experienced the Pareto Principal with your clients. The Pareto Principle is better known as the 80/20 rule. The 80/20 is overused, but it still holds true that 80% of your referrals will come from 20% of your clients.

From your vendor's perspective, you can be one of the top 20% of THEIR clients. Treat them well. When you have built strong interpersonal relationships with your vendors, many benefits and perks may come your way. Vendors can come with tips they see working well at other offices. They may bring gifts for the office. They may also be an insider as to which practices may be available for sale. When you have strong relationships with vendors, they may treat you like royalty at trades shows and introduce you to key players who can help you build your practice.

As with clients and staff, let vendors get to know you. We have discussed a lot about how to implement ROI-based marketing and KPI's. Well, you are your vendor's client. They want the same out of their relationship with you as you do with your clients.

Perhaps getting to know your vendors seems over the top. You will be surprised how much comes your way when you show interest in your vendors. You will suddenly find that when you need rush orders, they're available, or that they are more understanding when you need to stretch a payable one month.

Education and support also builds trust with your vendors, albeit in a different way. You can teach a vendor how you would like them to sell to you. When you openly share exactly what you are looking for when it comes to supplies and equipment and the outcomes you desire, the trust this builds with your vendors can lead you to their connections. Not to mention, you may be entitled to a few extra discounts (see Sell More, Spend Less).

***

All these tools and strategies to build trust and form high-value relationships can be fully executed doing one single thing--taking a genuine interest in others. This is not a *fake it until you make it* scenario. You either like people or you don't. Most communication is non-verbal, through tone, body language and presence, and any pandering will become immediately apparent.

This is one of the six ways to make people like you as written in Dale Carnegie's *How to Win Friends and Influence People*. If you haven't read this book, you need to go to Amazon, buy the Kindle copy and start reading it immediately. If you have already read this book, congratulations! Now read it again.

I have devoted a chapter in this book to relationships only to emphasize their importance in helping you to build your practice. This is an area where I have become a lifelong learner. The material never gets outdated, can be used in any situation at any time, and benefits me tremendously!

Are you fired up and ready to build? Here is a simple test for you. Answer the following question honestly:

Do you like people? Yes/No

***No** Answers*

You may be in for a tough road ahead of you. You are in the people business. To be successful in this industry, being around people is a critical component. If you have a negative attitude towards people, you will have a ton of difficulty being GENUINELY interested. If you feel like you're having to show up and be forced to talk to your patients, then you have a significant amount of work to do.

I am not referring to people who are introverted, because they can be coached. I am referring to doctors who genuinely do not like to be around other people. We have all met this type of person--the one who thinks they are Numero-Uno and that all others are there to serve them.

Sure, you can read all the books and learn all the tools to show an interest in other people. The issue is that you won't be authentic and that doesn't build trust. If you don't like people, you can bet they won't like you.

It's fine to want to enjoy alone time. I certainly love my ME time. It's also fine to enjoy being with people and then enjoy not being with them, too. But you must be able to enjoy the time when you are around people to be able to show genuine interest.

***Yes** Answers*

You are off to a great start. When you enjoy being around people in the moment, your interest will be genuine and authentic. This is a time where I like to be selfish. I know it sounds weird to say that having a genuine interest in people is selfish, but for me, I love to glean all I can from the people who surround me. I love to learn about their stories, their difficulties in life and how they've triumphed. That kind of stuff really fills my cup.

You may be thinking, *who has this much time on their hands? I need to be drilling and filing to pay the bills*. It doesn't take much time to build this connection--only a matter of seconds or minutes in most cases. You build consistency with each subsequent interaction. As the leader of your practice, your team will model your behavior. When you take a genuine interest, they will also. You will find that they are not only building relationships with your patients but may perhaps be better at it than you are!

I would like to share with you something I learned from Oprah:

"Fill your cup first and then fill others with your overflow."

This is the selfish part I was talking about. You can't really help others unless you have excess to give. If you're running on an empty emotional gas tank, it's difficult to be there for someone else. If you're somewhat selfish and fill your tank first, you will have a ton to give.

People will leave happier and healthier because they visited. After all, that is our job!

***

You have gained trust and interest while building rapport and furthering a high-value relationship with your clients. It's time to get your patients to value your offer. In my opinion, the most effective way to influence the value a patient feels you are offering is to teach them.

We communicate all our treatment plans in simple, transparent language using the PCSS or PROBLEM, CONSEQUENCE, SOLUTION, STOP technique. We train all our doctors to use it. It has doubled our treatment acceptance and minimized rejection. Our associate doctors swear buy it and we have developed an entire communications course around it.

The goal is to elicit a negative emotional response from the patient without being pushy or providing TMI. You want them to be as concerned about the problem as you would be. Teach them how to think about the problem using a simple PCSS format:

Here is a paraphrase of a teaching conversation I had with one of my patients:

> *REMEMBER: The message or words are read with the tone going on in your head. Given this read in a friendly and supportive tone vs. condescending or judgmental. I wrote this with kindness and support in mind.*

How do I do it?

I am sitting by the patient, facing the intra-oral picture on the screen and demonstrating the cracked tooth in plain sight.

Doctor: *John, do you see this crack here?*
Patient: *Yes, I do.*
Doctor: *Cracks spread. This will eventually spread into the nerve of your tooth, causing pain, infection and even tooth loss. In these situations, we place a cap/crown on the tooth that will hold it all together.*

STOP TALKING. PAUSE FOR AT LEAST FIVE SECONDS and resist the urge to break the silence with further education, or worse, begin talking them out of the ideal treatment by educating them on alternatives or statistics.

Yes. That's it. No fluff. Simple and transparent. Believe it or not, many patients convert without much more dialogue.

If they don't speak, simply ask, *"Do you have any questions?"*

Let the patient say the next words. This will be telling and will allow you to determine how to proceed next. For many patients at this stage, they have a crack, the consequence is obvious, and the solution is obvious. The intraoral photo has allowed them to co-diagnose, which is important.

The patient may be tense or concerned because you have elicited an emotional response from them (negative emotion, which is concern associated with pain, infection or tooth loss). They need to understand and feel the consequence, so it serves as motivation to solve their problem. This is not trickery or a scare tactic. It is simply transparently and intelligently sharing the potential consequences of not treating the tooth.

My job is to help patients understand the consequences of their problems and what the worst-case scenario would be. I then give them the choice to avoid the worst case in a way every single one of them will unmistakably understand. This is preventative dentistry.

Here is a significantly different presentation style. I hear this style a lot from doctors with low treatment acceptance numbers:

***Doctor**: Mr. Smith, your tooth is cracked (no visual aid to demonstrate that it is, in fact, cracked). Right now, the crack looks like it is above the gum line. The likelihood of that crack spreading is about 50%. These cracks tend to introduce bacteria into your nerve which can cause* *inflammation. The crack may result in a vertical root fracture, which would require that we remove the tooth, or it could spread to the nerve, which would require a root canal. We need to crown this tooth so that doesn't happen.*

The doctor then proceeds to make matters worse by busting out a pen and paper and drawing the problem and the solution. He continues to provide TMI by launching into the process of doing a crown--or worse, drawing out a variety of crown margins.

By that time, the patient is so tuned out, bored, confused or worried about the root canal they just heard about, the doctor has lost the patient's attention. Remember that confused minds don't buy! Does this sound like you? Well it was me in my first few months of practice. Fortunately, I had an assistant who was honest with me and said:

***Assistant**: Dr. Justin, your patients don't understand what you're saying.*
***Me**: Which ones?*
***Assistant**: All of them. You're talking over their heads. They ask me a million questions every time you leave the room.*

I knew right then I had to find a better way. I did, and as a result, I increased my conversion percentage, as well as saving SO MUCH TIME in presenting treatment options. I'm illustrating this because you can build value through education, and most importantly by using language that speaks to your clients.

PROBLEM | CONSEQUENCE | SOLUTION | STOP

Education for a patient in a chair is much different than the education you received in dental school. They don't care about most of the technical details you need to know to fix the crack in the tooth. They just want to know enough information to make an informed decision.

When you think about both types of conversations, which one do you think builds more trust? The one where we are having a simple and transparent conversation or the one where the dentist is talking so far over the patient's head that the patient now believes the dentist is trying to pull one over on them or sell them? Or worse, the patient tunes out completely because they feel incompetent or intimidated?

After the initial PCSS presentation, which takes a matter of seconds, you can begin a two-way conversation lead by the patient's objections and questions. Questions are either objections in disguise or a desire to collect more information or clarity. At this stage, feel free to use statistics (quote university studies), analogies, cartoons and other tools to drive the point home based on the patient's specific questions--but not before they ask.
If there is no response, simply ask if they have any questions.
REMEMBER: Educate to inform. Don't confuse them with too much chatter and technical jargon. Keep the

conversation simple and elicit the emotional response associated with the consequence of no treatment.

Examples of questions/objections:

- What is a crown?
- How much does it cost?
- Are there any other options?
- It doesn't hurt or cause me pain right now.

Each of these objections or questions can be managed several different ways. Here is how we handle such questions:

What is a crown? A crown is X, Y, Z (use visual aid and show before/after of successful cases)

How much does it cost? I am just straight up here. No beating around the bush. The cost of the crown is $X. The *Good News* is your insurance (for those with insurance) will typically cover a portion of that. This is a better way to position it as opposed to saying, "Your insurance ONLY covers a portion of the cost."

Are there any other options? Yes. There are other options. You can remove the old filling from this tooth (if amalgam is present) and place a new filling. It is cheaper and quicker, but it doesn't seal the crack, which still has the potential to spread and cause pain and infection. We can do this or the crown. We will support whatever decision you make*.

It doesn't hurt or cause me pain right now. I am glad it's not causing you pain. You're very lucky, because many patients with a cracked tooth are in pain. Cracks typically don't hurt until it's too late, and at that point, the tooth is infected or needs to be removed.

*The goal is to help the patient understand the other option is inferior to the crown, as well to inform them that if they choose that option, we will deliver the treatment with no judgment and only support. This is important! Although we want them to do the crown because we know it's the most durable option and the one which will solve their problem long-term, we also don't want them to leave the practice because they feel we are pushing a crown on them. Do the filling and later you can recommend the crown again.

Please don't get too caught up on the exact words here. The bottom line is, we need to communicate simply and transparently to increase treatment acceptance. Our full training involves the initial presentation by the RDA or RDH (address Chief Complaint and use of PCSS to discuss clinical findings), the hand-off from RDA/RDH to the doctor (using PCSS, further deepening concern).

Then the handoff from the doctor or RDA/RDH to the treatment coordinator/front end team member (using verbiage to create urgency and get the appointment scheduled today). This sounds complex, but with the right training, it becomes second nature and it's quite easy. This also feels very rewarding, because patients like how simple it is to understand.

The takeaway here is that when you involve the patient in their education about the treatment, they feel authorship and ownership. They have the control and they will believe there is value in the treatment plan you're presenting.

Let's face it. Most people do not want dentistry--especially when problems are not causing patients discomfort now. Our job is to show them the Problem, Consequence and Solution and then Stop talking. Then we answer all the necessary questions.

You don't have to take my word for it. A recent periodical reported the key to dental case acceptance:[iii]

"Patients will say yes more often if they think their dentist is interested in their well-being and is a trusted partner and not a condescending teacher or salesperson. A trusted advisor does not tell patients what they "need," what they "ought to do," or what they "have to do." Dentists should ask questions first, then devise a treatment plan that addresses each patient's situation."

Bottom line: People don't care how much you know until they know how much you care!

An important part of the process in educating patients is asking questions. You now have two choices:

You can go in guns-blazing with information. You can overload them and try to teach them to be dentists while in your chair.

You can ask questions.

If you ask questions, you're going to have a much better chance at developing a high-trust relationship. Before you start talking and diagnosing, it's important to ask questions and train your team to ask the right questions. As mentioned above, there is an RDA/RDH component that was left out to keep the process simpler. We also have specific PCSS language for each problem we present.

***

In short:

- Address patient's chief complain using PCSS. If you don't get the chief complaint out of the way, they will be thinking about this throughout the entire process.

- Address all other findings using PCSS.

- Allow patients to guide the remainder of the treatment presentation. For those not engaging, simply ask if they have any questions. If they don't ask you they will ask your staff. This is the importance of staff training!

- Create a sense of urgency prior to the patient leaving the operatory and book their appointment right then.

- Practice, Practice, Practice.

A study at the University College London[iv] observed that 66 days is the average time needed for a habit to become automatic, where automaticity is described as, *I do this without having to consciously remember*. Learn AND practice the PCSS for 66 days so this becomes automatic for you and your team. Then watch your treatment acceptance soar!

More on Relationships and Trust

The essence of a strong trust relationship starts with authenticity. Part of demonstrating authenticity is showing your human side. This can be a very difficult element for a lot of doctors. We have this persona of strength, knowledge and reliability. We forget that trust is also built through vulnerability.

Showing some vulnerability is not having a total breakdown in front of your client, unloading all your personal problems or sobbing uncontrollably. Being vulnerable in a professional environment is more about showing that you're human.

For example, if you missed a treatment outcome or if you make an error in billing and it's your fault, then admit it.

It's perfectly fine to say, 'I'm sorry. That was our mistake." Don't try to make excuses or justify the problem. Just look the patient in the eyes and say, *"I'm sorry. That must be frustrating. We'll help you fix this."*

This is empathy as well as vulnerability.

The vulnerable part is admitting the mistake. The good news is that mistakes don't happen very often. Just accept responsibility when they do happen.

The easiest way to be vulnerable with your patients is to let them into your life. We discussed this at length earlier in the chapter and it is worth mentioning again. The chances are high that you and your clients will have something in common. Some of your patients will share a little about what interests them. They might tell you a little about their family or what they do for a living. You might find that you're from the same community or that your kids play the same sports. The sharing is also a demonstration of vulnerability.

Many doctors have a hard time with this and insist on being relentlessly formal about their practice. The misperception is that this vulnerability somehow takes away from their credibility. The truth is that it doesn't. Your clients come to you because you're a competent doctor. Your vulnerability makes you more relatable.

I understand this is difficult. I continue to work on becoming vulnerable every day of my career. I pursue improvement instead of perfection. I will occasionally share a challenge I am having with my kids with some of my patients who also have kids. Sometimes they offer advice and I learn from them. The point is that I open up a little about my life and involve my clients in my journey. One of the benefits is that we both feel great as a result. The other end result is that my treatment acceptance and rebooking rates go up.

Obviously, you won't have time for in-depth conversations every time, but the more you have, the more effective you will become. Ask about your patients' lives. People love to talk about themselves. Simply using one's name correctly and often perks up their ears. That's a great place start. For a simple tool to help you think about how to start a meaningful conversation, refer to Dale Carnegie's Conversation Stack below. If you are good at carrying on a conversation, this may come naturally. If you struggle with this, check it out.

Name Plate	Introduction	❑ Ask their name ❑ Introduce yourself
House of Your Dreams	Living Situation	❑ *"Where are you from?"* ❑ *"How long have you lived there?"* ❑ *"What'd you like about living in that city,town,region etc...?"* ❑ *"Would you move back if you had the chance?"*
Your Family	Family Situation	❑ *"Do you have any siblings?"* ❑ *"Oh really, how many?"* ❑ *"Do you have any pets? What are their names?"* ❑ *"Does your family still live in your hometown?"*
Workers Glove	Working Situation	❑ *"Are you a student?"* ❑ *"What do you do for a living?"* ❑ *"Do you like your job?"* ❑ *"How long have you been at that company/organization?"*
Pink 747	Travel Interests	❑ *"Do you like to travel?"* ❑ *"Where have you been?"* ❑ *"Would you go there again?"* ❑ *"What was your favorite part about the trip?"*
Tennis Racket	Hobbies	❑ *"What do you like to do for fun?"* ❑ *"Do you play sports?"* ❑ *"What's you favorite sports team?"* ❑ *"What's your favorite TV show, book, movie, etc...?"*
Goal Posts	Aspirations	❑ *"What do you want to be when you 'grow up'?"* ❑ *"What's a personal goal that people would be surprised to hear?"* ❑ *"What's your #1 goal to achieve this year?"*

Then answer the same questions about yourself. That's all it really takes. It is not necessary to go too long or deep. When you commit to getting to know your patients while at the same time becoming vulnerable, you will find that the conversation becomes easier. You will also find that your relationships with your clients build from visit to visit. Imagine that? The conversation grows as the relationship grows.

But there's more! You will also observe that this leadership by example will get your staff chatting up the patients. They'll model your behavior and take care of the conversations so you can come in spend a few minutes building rapport or connecting and begin treatment. There is no need to rush in or out. The bottom line is to be vulnerable and create a culture of openness in your office.

As I mentioned in the *WHY* chapter, one of the reasons I became a dentist was for the income and lifestyle I thought it would afford me. After all these years, I've learned that money is only one piece of the puzzle. We spend countless hours at work, and I've learned that it is critical to my personal well-being to find happiness and joy in it. I found myself anxiously waiting until 5 p.m. or the weekend because I hadn't established dentistry as a place where I could fulfill my higher purpose. After all, they're just teeth, right?

Wrong! We can be and do so much more than just dentists clocking in and out. I found a home in this profession because I ascribed a meaning to it that was deeper than monetary goals. I realized that I could really do some good and help people. I consider it my personal mission to give people the best possible experiences and get them the treatment they deserve. I pursue continuing education so I can give more and help more. Most importantly for me, however, is that I've created leadership in our team and with my patients and have become a source of positive influence inside and outside of the office. Our group vision is to have a positive impact on our team, patients and community.

***

All this discussion about soft skills like building relationships, communication, building trust and being vulnerable comes down to this: Approximately 70% of people experience some level of dental fear (Shulte, 2013)[v]. This is important for those in your practice to acknowledge because the way you address this level of fear or mistrust will either help or hurt your KPI's.

MORE IMPORTANTLY...seven out of 10 people are delaying or avoiding coming to your practice to get the treatments they need because of their fear. If you've heard differently, that's okay. Let's not get hung up on the exact number. Just acknowledge there are a lot of people afraid to walk through your front door.
What's disappointing is that I don't find these figures surprising at all. Let's face it. The overall perception of dentistry is that we bring pain and discomfort. From that perspective, I understand it. Why would anyone willingly go to see any professional knowing that they were going to hurt them?

Another interesting note from Schultz:

> *"About 30% of all of our anxious patients reported to have experienced traumatic dental treatments during childhood dental visits as a cause for their [dental fear]. Reasons are thought to be pain experienced during these treatments and/or brutal and insensitive conduct by the dentist. Another third of the interviewed patients refer to scary accounts of others, frequently their own parents, as the starting point for their fears. For the remaining third, there do not seem to be any obvious causes for their [dental fear]."*

Knowing most patients are anxious, please take a minute to gain their trust prior to starting treatment:

> *"Mr./Mrs. Patient, I know it can be nerve-wracking to be here, but I want you to know I do this all day every day and I am good at what I do. I also want you to know that you are in charge and in control. You can stop me at any point if you are overwhelmed. Do you have any questions before we start, or would it help if we vocalized what we are doing through the treatment?"*

The other source of mistrust from patients is when they receive unexpected treatment recommendations. No two dentists are going to see the same diagnosis all the time. Consider this tale of two dentists. One dentist started his practice after dental school and had very limited dental education following his post-secondary. The second

dentist spent hundreds of hours in continuing education and became renowned for her skills.
The first dentist completes his checkup and verifies no cavities and no cancer. The patient leaves after a $200 cleaning. The second dentist sees the same patient and observes a number of cracks, several crowns for the back teeth, suggests braces to broaden the patient's smile and recommends a few veneers. The second dentist also observes the signs of parafunction and can see issues with chewing and grinding. The same patient gets a treatment recommendation of over $50,000 and leaves with a feeling of doubt. This is an extreme example, and as mentioned above, there is something to be said about phasing treatment, but you get the idea.

Why would two dentists have two radically different diagnoses on the same patient? To the patient, dentists are not that different from each other, so the inconsistent treatments creates dramatic mistrust. We know as dentists that when we learn more, we see more. It makes sense to us that the diagnoses could easily be different.

The same goes for us in other areas of our lives. If our car needs work, we will either

Always go to the same trustworthy mechanic, taking all of his recommendations because of the relationship we have with him.

Shop around until we get the lowest price, and more importantly, find a mechanic we think won't swindle us.

Either way, it comes down to trust. Building high-value trust relationships with our clients has never been more important in building a successful practice.

I used the example above because many patients seek second opinions. We see these in our office all the time. When a patient asks for a second opinion, they are really indicating they want the treatment, just not from that dentist."

So instead, they show up on your doorstep. There are a variety of reasons that the patient may choose to seek a second opinion--primarily trust and finances. If you are the dentist who inherits a patient with a comprehensive treatment plan or one you disagree with, please remember you have options on how you can deal with that. It's not necessary to try and be the hero and come to the rescue by throwing the other doc under the bus through disapproval of his/her work. Be wary of using words like *that's aggressive* or *I disagree* or promoting yourself with phrases like *I'm a conservative dentist*.

Simply acknowledge that someone else has received more training than you, sees what you don't see or has a different practice philosophy. You can simply recognize that and let the patient know

> *"Mr./Mrs. Patient, I have reviewed the plan and have a -recommendation of my own."*

Simply present yours without belittling your colleagues'. The same goes for sub-par treatment you may see. Give your colleagues the benefit of the doubt. I am not suggesting anyone ignore abuse or unnecessary treatment recommendations. I am simply saying that we ought to uplift one another for the benefit of the profession. I hope you can see that keeping this mindset over a long period of time will benefit the entire profession. Believe it or not, a diplomatic response significantly increases patients' trust in you. People may judge you for speaking negatively of others.

If you feel compelled to share your feelings about some else's work with someone, simply reach out the doctor themselves and let them know directly. This is an opportunity either to help someone else or learn something new--both are wins for you. Approach sharing your thoughts in a kind, friendly and diplomatic manner vs. like approaching one's enemy. We are all in this together. The benefit to you is the ability to practice in a profession in which patients' trust is increasing.

REMEMBER: Everyone is trying their best. Their best may not yet be quite as good as yours. With new knowledge, training, encouragement and practice, they will get there. They may just need a helping hand.

Ideas to Remember

- You need to give before you get.
- The basis of a good relationship is to treat people well, let them get to know you, get to know them, don't be pushy and provide education and support.
- Take a genuine interest in people.
- People value ideas more when they feel they have been educated. Problem | Consequence | Solution | Stop
- Patients are more likely to accept a treatment when they've participated in the diagnosis.
- Be vulnerable. The magic happens outside of your comfort zone.
- Case acceptance is on the other side of trust. Trust is created with positive experiences, simplicity and transparency, compounded with consistency.

CHAPTER SIX

Be a Leader, Not a Boss

"It is a terrible thing to look over your shoulder when you are trying to lead -- and find no one there."
~Franklin D. Roosevelt

I want to cut straight to the point. I don't think anyone wants to be told what to do. If they do, they clearly have no real desire to be involved in the task.

It has been a long time since I had a boss. I have been an entrepreneur for most of my career. For the time I spent as an employee, I didn't feel like a really had a boss. I always felt I was a leader, even when I was in a subordinate role.

I have worked tirelessly toward enlightenment about what leadership really is. I have spent well over a million dollars on training and development. I find it difficult to sum up all I have learned over the past 10 years. Who I am today is not exactly who I was 10 years ago, and 10 years from now, I will not be exactly who I am today. Why? In order to do more, you must become more.

"Who do I need to become?"

When you think about what they do, anyone can be a boss. When I let my imagination run, the vision I get is that the boss sits at the desk, feet up, a cigar in his mouth, shouting orders to his subordinates. The boss directs people to *go here and do that* and points a finger at everyone when things don't work out as planned.

The leader is out there in the trenches. A leader is doing more than setting an example, he/she is also creating an environment where everyone else can shine. In many ways, the leader's role is to build other leaders.

That's why I included Roosevelt's quote at the beginning of this chapter. The biggest take away I can give you is to find out who you need to become so that when you look back over your shoulder, you have a team accompanying you.

One of my expectations of my team is that they control the energy they bring with them to the office every day. If they're not, they're bringing in all the chaos from getting the kids off to school or the argument they just had with their spouse. The fact that there's something going on in their lives takes them out of the space where they need to be in order to serve our patients. They are just not ready to deliver a great experience. It affects everyone in the office through what current neuroscience research calls *emotional contagion.* Their non-verbal communication will send the message that they are in a bad place. Life is unpredictable and we don't always have a perfect start to our day, but when we show up for work, we have to hang that up at the door, walk in and be ready to serve.

I ask myself, "Who do I need to become to be the leader they deserve?" Since I expect my team to control the energy they bring, I must control my energy. The leader is also a doer.

I have been fortunate in my career to have had the opportunity to speak with some pretty successful people and great leaders--people at the top of their games, professionally and personally, many millionaires and even a couple of billionaires. Here's one thing they all have in common. They all have a morning routine. They start their day with an anchoring process that sets the stage for what is to come. For some it lasts only a few minutes, and others up to an hour—but they all do it. I have learned to start my day with intention and strength. This gives me the push I need to start my day with my best foot forward.

Here's what I do:

My morning routine lasts about 90 minutes and is completely technology free, except during the exercise component where I usually listen to a podcast or music, making sure my phone is on airplane mode to prevent any distractions from dings and pings. No emails, no texts and no social media.

- Drink 26 oz of water straight away.
- Exercise intensely for a minimum of 20 minute (I prefer H.I.I.T. training--High Intensity Interval Training).
- Gratitude Journal
- Meditate for 10 minutes (longer if I am feeling into it)
- Learn: Business, psychology, leadership, neuroscience or personal development, typically in the form of a podcast, audio book or scientific literature.
- Set the intention for the day and review my high-value tasks and deliverables.

I start the morning by answering the following questions in my journal:

- What am I most happy about right now?
- What am I most excited about?
- What am I most proud of right now?
- What am I grateful for in my life right now?
- What am I enjoying most in my life right now?
- What am I committed to in my life right now?
- Who do I love? Who loves me? What do I love most about them?

No matter what seems to be happening that day, answering some or all of these questions always raises my mood and enables me to bring the best possible energy to the office.

When I set these intentions every day, I can be the example my team needs to see. This is about showing people instead of telling them how to behave. Teach them how to think. That's what you're doing. You're living into it.

A big part of making my practices successful is that we build WOW experiences for our patients. Crafting the actual experiences themselves could be an entire separate book. The leadership lesson is: who do I need to become so my team is empowered to create *wow* experiences?

Show up to the office with the intention of creating a *wow* experience. Create one yourself as an example. Then show your team how that's done.

The alternative is to be a boss. Tell them what to do, watch them fail and then reprimand them and eventually let them go. Lather, rinse, repeat. People generally don't want to do things incorrectly. They want to excel at their jobs, find joy in them and be rewarded. Give your employees that opportunity by being leading by example and stepping out of your comfort zone. Asking people to do things you're unwilling to do is not leadership. This doesn't mean that you need to learn to answer the phones and enter patients into your practice management software. It does mean that if you expect them to do their best, you also do your best. If you expect them to treat your patients like gold, you do the same.

So... who do you need to become?

***

"I used to lead by example but
it was too much work."

Leadership is more about showing than it is telling. As the leader in our respective practices we have to BE the example before our patients, team, vendors or anyone else with whom we choose to build a relationship will follow in our footsteps. That's why I get a chuckle from the comic strip above. This is exactly what I imagine working for a huge, faceless corporation would be like. We are lucky to be in a position to positively influence so many people on a day-to-day basis. Being the example is hard work--not just because we have to step out of our comfort zone for many reasons, but also because we have to do it every day all day. It is not easy, but it is worth it!

I have also implemented several daily routines.

- Morning routine (listed above)
- Transition routine.
- Clear desk routine.

Each serves as a valuable *reset button* in my mind and enables me to close the task I was working on and open the next task with a clear mind and intention.

Transition Routine

I transition myself between tasks and patients, as well as different settings or environments.

Examples:

Patient to patient: I repeat to myself, *"Presence, efficiency and the particular procedure into which I am walking (Example: root canal)."* This allows me to release from the last patient encounter and give the next patient the attention they deserve. The best gift we can give our patients is total focus and presence. As well it transitions me from the previous procedure the to one I will be now performing.

From the parking lot to the office doors: I repeat to myself, FUN, LEADERSHIP and PRODUCTIVITY.
Between tasks: I release myself from the last tasks and set the intention for the new one.

In my driveway before I enter my home from a workday: *Your family deserves the best of you not what is left of you. Nothing is more important than your family.* This puts things in perspective and allows me to be present with my loved ones versus coming home from a stressful day and brushing them off or being stuck in my own head.

Clear Desk Routine

At the end of the day, I complete any unfinished or lingering tasks to free myself of them. Of course, I don't address anything that would require an all-nighter or days to complete.

> ***WARNING***
>
> *Beware of excuses which may upset your routines.*
>
> *"I am too tired."*
>
> *"I already had a productive day."*
>
> *"I can just add this task to tomorrow's To-Do List."*
>
> *This type of self-talk will pile up. Instead, just get it done and clear your desk. Don't allow today's work to carry over into tomorrow. It will only create more stress.*

All of these rituals/habits/routines put me in a positive mindset and enables me to be more present in the moment.

The sense of accomplishment increases my confidence. The tank is on empty at the start of every day and my confidence and positivity are neutral. It's the moments of the day that either *add to* or *subtract from* our confidence and positivity. When I begin the day with such powerful routines, I am building up a surplus of these high-performance emotions and can easily build on them or withstand a few minor blows from the events of the day.

The goal is to transition from activity to activity without loss of enthusiasm. Hit the reset button along the way and build your high-performance practice.

I recognize this is easier said than done. I slip up often. Life, dentistry and business are stressful and there is no shortage of fires to put out. You are so much more prepared to handle those tough moments when you have great habits and rituals to back you up. Perfection is not the goal--it's progress. Anything is better than nothing at all. In fact, just the intention is a good start, as it demonstrates awareness and a shift in mindset.

Don't delay, get started today!

I mentioned that I transition myself from the parking lot to the office doors. Priming myself to have fun, be a leader and be productive. As soon as I walk through those doors, I say hi to each team member. I try to chat with everyone briefly and ask them how they're doing, or perhaps how their previous night went. In other words, I take a genuine interest in my staff. They are important to me, and I know how important it is for them to chat and connect (remember—high-value trust relationships!). This also allows me to gauge how everyone is doing and diffuse any landmines early on.

For example, if a team member is off and moody, I simply say,

> *"You don't seem like yourself today. You don't have to talk about it. Just know that if there is anything I or the team can do to help you, let us know."*

My team knows if they are having an off day, the best thing they can do is say,

"Team, I'm not 100% today. Bear with me, please."

Vulnerability is a strength!

When your team recognizes your leadership, they respond kindly and launch into support mode when fellow team members are having a bad day. The fact that they can comfortably share without fear of judgment speaks to the office culture and values. This is so important. When someone feels they can be open and honest, it significantly improves overall mood and it's all uphill from there.

I do my best to set my intentions, control my attitude and set up my day for success. On a bad day, I let my team know in the same way I expect of them. Maybe I'm not having the best day, but I will set my intentions and I will do my best to be present for everyone. This level of vulnerability creates instant compassion and connection with your team. I wouldn't be much of a leader if I didn't share that with my team and be the example. One tool I have implemented which I believe has had a tremendous impact on all of our relationships is the *team huddle*.

The huddle is designed to set the intention. We start by identifying any landmines that may come up during the day, like a scheduled appointment with a difficult client. Ultimately, the huddle is practice, preparation and a rehearsal for the day. When we identify any bottlenecks or landmines that may cause stress or disrupt our day, we can ALL address how we are going to deal with them and mitigate the stress before it even happens. In addition, we discuss the production goals, same day treatment conversion and other matters related to the numbers.

The last two pieces of the huddle are gratitude and a quote of the day. Everyone is asked to share three things for which they are grateful. They don't have to share if they prefer not to. Simply thinking of being grateful for health, having a wonderful family or not having to work outside in the cold is just as important as voicing them aloud--whatever gratitude means to them.

Our *Huddle Lead* then shares a quote for inspiration or significance. We discuss it and then close out our huddle. That process in itself tends to change attitudes and sets the intention for the day. It also aligns us with our goals and touches on how we will get there. After all, the only two things any person can control is their attitude and their activity. None of this magic happens until we *be* the example we would like to see in others.

So back to the little comic above. I wish this was just a joke mocking reality. Sadly, I have seen this in many practices at varying levels. The truth is, leading by example this is hard work. It takes a ton of energy and effort. We all know that our brains are hardwired to resist change. That's why habits are so powerful at making us efficient machines.

This is important: Staying the same and grinding through the stress of an unsuccessful practice is just as stressful and difficult as it is to work on changing yourself to become better and stronger. If you're going to go through the pain and suffering anyway, why not choose the latter? My sincerest hope is that I am able to give you the push you need to step up and step out of your comfort zone.

The installation of this habit is going to make you a better leader. It will result in increased productivity, and even if it doesn't, you're going to learn something from the process.

You can either work through the pain of success or live with the pain of regret. I am not telling you it will be easy. I am just telling you it will be worth it.

***

If you agree that good leadership is about being the example, you should also recognize that empowering people by teaching them is also a demonstration of what it means to be a leader and not a boss. As I was starting my career and even into acquiring my first few practices, I noticed a trend:

TELL | SHOW | DO

This is a very widely accepted means of training and education. Do you remember how you were trained? You were most likely trained using *Tell, Show, Do* and were probably taught this in your pediatric classes.

Tell them what you are going to do.
Show them how to do it.
Go ahead and *do* it.

For example, when I had a young patient, I would TELL them, "We are going to take this air gun and we're going to spray your tooth with it." Then I would SHOW them by spraying on their hand. Lastly, I would DO it.

My offices had acceptable results using that method of training with our team. They were lacking the *wow* results I was looking for.

You have probably had similar experiences in your practice. You attend a weekend course and come back with a few amazing ideas you want to implement. So, you put together a presentation for your team and say, *Boom! This is what we're doing.* Then your team thinks to themselves, *all right, let's just not do anything for the next month and he'll forget about it.* Or I would speak with my receptionist, let her know we need to convert more new patients to butts in the chair and give her a script and the method to do so. A week later, no change. Sound familiar? That was happening in my practices.

That's when I really looked inward and thought, *is this being a leader or a boss?* I felt that when I used *Tell, Show, Do* with my team, I was being a boss and not a leader.

> *Special Tip*
>
> *It is a great idea to take your team members with you when you attend a course. They feel immediately bought-in, are empowered by the education and experience the same buzz you feel after coming back from a CE course.*

That is when I re-tooled my approach and implemented:

Teach | Show | Explain

Teach, Show and Explain is an adaptation of the former.

Teach - When we educate, we empower
Show - For understanding
Explain - Explain the *why*, the objective and the value

This process is based on leading by example and has uncovered two important embedded values: clear communication and collaborative teamwork. Put another way, when we fail to adequately explain the *why* (of a task, an objective, etc.) or include our team or clients in the process, we fail to get buy-in from them simply because we are not buying into our own value system. Is that clear?

Let me explain this another way. When you are able to get buy-in, you are creating authorship (or ownership, or any other possessive word you prefer to use here). I have to assume you have the right team. If not, please don't worry. We're going to talk about building your dream team in Chapter Seven.

Back to authorship. This is huge. Hear them out. List the problems they come up with and listen to their solutions.

Here's an example:

If I was to approach my team with the idea that we want to deliver great service to our patients. Is that a goal we all share? *Yes.*

> *Doctor: Our intake of patient information is taking three times as long as it should, and our exits are taking two to three times longer. We're sending the message to our patients that we don't value their time. Can you shed some light on why that's happening?*

This is an incredibly effective means to empower your team. They feel heard, validated and are now a part of the process. Keep in mind, this only works if they see you as their leader not their boss. There is no trust if your team never comments or contributes and or you're the only one talking. Meetings between people who trust each other may have some conflict and straight talk and is usually followed by resolution and execution. That's building a high-performance practice!

> *Team: What can we do to fix this? Do we need a new form? Should we complete appointments earlier? Should we collect information at the beginning of the appointment versus the end because people would rather leave right away?*
>
> *Doctor: Thanks so much for suggesting these solutions. Now please go ahead pick the one you want, and at the end of the day, let me know what you've decided.*

Once decided, a documented protocol can be created and used for training. If you disagree with your team members' choice, do you have any data or a good reason to object? Often, it's the need to be in control which causes the itch to disagree. Instead, perhaps allow it to roll out for a two-to-four-week period and assess the results. Are patient wait times down? Quicker exits taking place? If so, leave it alone. If not, go back and try the next solution.

In this example, we taught our team the meaning behind the numbers, showed them the importance and then explained what we wanted them to do. This sharing process allows validation. It allows people to be heard and empowered. They author the solution, at least part of it, and you get to choose which way to go. This is kind of like a choose-your-own-adventure in the office. You might have heard several new ideas, and now you can roll out what you want.

This demonstrates the difference between dictating and co-creating. You could dictate that you want the team to collect all the information at the beginning of the appointment or finish the appointments a little sooner.

However, I have seen a drastic improvement in the performance of my practices because we co-create. I have a better relationship with my team and my team builds a better relationship with our patients. Depending on the size of your office or number of offices, you are typically relying on your A-players for feedback and not the bottom 10% who prefer to complain. One way or another, they all affect our bottom line.

I have one last burning revelation about authorship and co-creating....

Are you ready?

People default to their highest level of training. Always. That is why it is so important to TEACH | SHOW | EXPLAIN so you effectively raise the level of training or education in your team AND in your patients. Habit is hard to break. Most of us are too lazy to do the work required to break old habits or old ways of doing things. We have all heard the phrase, *Old habits die hard*. Most people will spend a ton of energy fighting to stay there.

The Solution: *Teach, Show, Explain* and Authorship. Unless people understand WHY it is important to make a change and are given an opportunity to co-author the solution, the likelihood of lasting change is slim.

Co-creating is not a single event but a constant effort. To lead by example also includes YOU! Can you imagine how disruptive you would be if the objective your team decided was to finish appointments earlier and it's time to go to the next operatory and you're lagging, taking your time or flat out not listening? You send the message that their decisions aren't important. This process works well but requires you to be the example.

My wish for you is that you recognize the power these strategies will give you to grow your practice to whatever size you desire. Do you want a profitable seven-figure practice? Multiple practices? Perhaps you want more time with your family? A few days off?

I am not saying it will be easy. It will be hard. And it will be worth it.

***

This chapter's entire discussion about leading by example comes down to the most important activity in your practice—to show your clients and staff what customer service is.

Customer service needs to be demystified a little bit and simplified a lot. There are literally hundreds (maybe even more) of different tactics you can use to demonstrate customer service. I have simplified it down to this one thing: good customer service is about how you make the other person feel. Maya Angelou says:

> *"I've learned that people will forget what you said, people will forget what you did, but people will never forget how you made them feel."*

How many times have you been running from one appointment to the next and when you rush in to the operatory, your patient comments, "Wow. You must be really busy today?" The comment is fairly innocent but think about how that patient must feel as you rush in and rush out of the room.

I completely understand there are those days when you are booked solid and your schedule seems to be stacked against you. I know because I have been there. Making your clients or teammates feel important is not a sometime thing. It's an all-the-time thing, and it's up to you to show your clients and team what customer service is. When those moments come up and you catch yourself rushing, here are a couple of things you can do:

Respond that yes, your office is busy today, but that you plan for these days and leave plenty of time so you're able to take care of each patient to make sure you're thorough. This acknowledgment and reassurance will go a long way to leaving your patient feeling good about their visit.

Stop and pause for a few seconds. Transition yourself as described earlier and move on. You can be efficient while you are in their mouth, but you need to be attentive and deliberate as you enter and exit the operatory. Don't rush in and out. That's the patient's first and last impression.

Here are a few other ideas we have implemented in our practices that have drastically improved our customer service:

Smile - Smiling is so simple it is often overlooked. The action of smiling has an effect on your patients and staff and uplifts your mood in the moment. By my estimation the cost-benefit of a smile is about 1:1 Million.

Adjust your tone - The tone of your voice says more about what you're saying than the words you choose. If you're tone is anxious, the people around you will feel anxious. People feel calm and confident when you share that tone.

Meet in the lobby - One activity I have adopted is to meet my patients in the lobby whenever possible and greet them with a bottle of water. This type of reception has a much better impact than walking into the operatory staring at a chart and not even looking up at the patient.

Why You Should Care

Software Advice reviewed a survey of 817 people to understand how they use on-line review sites to evaluate medical practitioners.[vi] They reported that 82% of patients use review sites to view or post comments about healthcare staff.

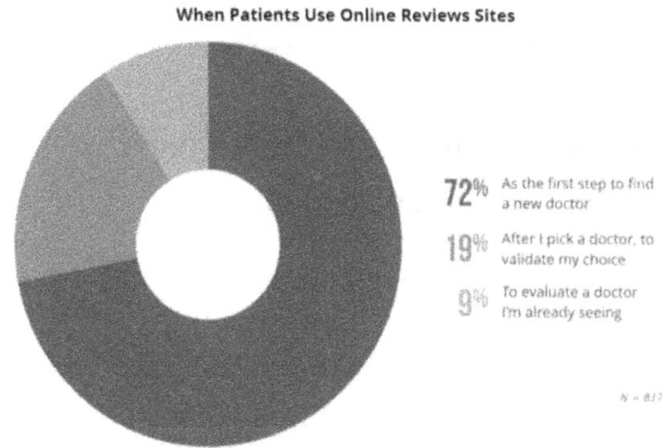

What you should take from this is that your on-line reputation precedes you. What is the current state of your online reputation? Is it good, bad or non-existent? In any case, reviews leave a real and tangible effect on the success of your practice and are dependent on your level of customer service.

If that isn't enough for you, Dentistry IQ reported findings[vii] about where patients went to review information:

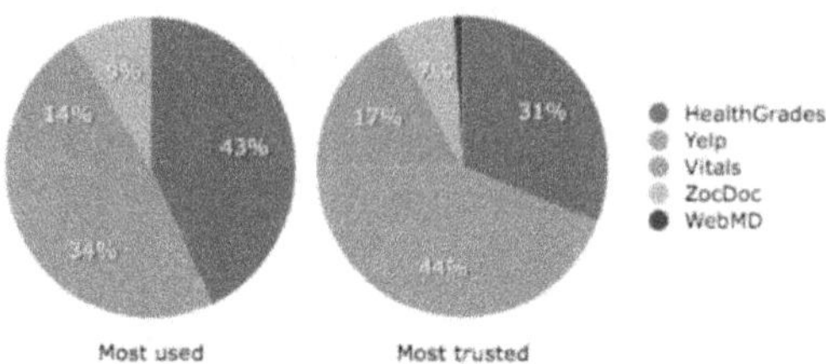

HealthGrades was the most used review website, albeit marginally, Yelp was the most trusted site for reviews of healthcare providers. Google and RateMDs have also become significant trusted, much-used review sources.

All of this links back to how you build your customer-service culture. Do you tell it or live it?

***

I want to apologize to you. Up until this point in the chapter, I feel I have been misleading. I have made it sound like I have absolutely everything buttoned up and my leadership is perfect. The truth is, I'm not perfect. In fact, my leadership skills are far where I want them to be. I often make mistakes, but here are two reasons I've found success:

My ability to be humble and vulnerable, taking accountability for my mistakes vs. pointing the finger or making excuses

I acknowledge my mistake/failure, learn, reset and quickly move on.

I have come a long way yet find that I still have lots of room to improve. Along my journey, I've learned that I always need to continually seek new ways to develop my leadership qualities.

Take on this Task

What are the 10-20 items you want to accomplish as a leader? Take a moment and break out a blank piece of paper. Lean back, close your eyes and take five deep breaths, in through your nose and out through your mouth. Now grab your pen and simply start writing everything that is coming into your mind that you want to accomplish as a leader. List all the words and phrases you can think of. Take as long as you need and stop when you feel you are done.

Close your eyes again and take another five deep breaths. Quickly read through your entire list, saying the words out loud. Really feel what you're reading. Immediately afterward, circle the words or phrases which jump out at you. Decide to take steps over the next 12 months to improve the highlighted areas.

How did you like that exercise? I hope you took it all the way through, and you now have a list of initiatives you can act on right now.

I would like to take a moment and share with you a few of the leadership initiatives I am working on.

Communicating Clearly

Merriam-Webster[viii] defines communication as *a process by which information is exchanged between individuals through a common system of symbols, signs or behavior*. I would like to add that *the message is understood* to this definition. That's the key piece I continuously work on and improve. I am very conscious about thinking before I speak, using an appropriate tone, carefully choosing my language, controlling the pace, being aware of my non-verbal communication and resisting the desire to interrupt, as a few examples.

The other part of this definition I love is *behavior*. Our behavior communicates quite a bit more than the symbols or signs we use to communicate. Hopefully, this is starting to sound familiar to you as you recall all of the discussion about leading by example.

Support

This can be a very vague subject. What does *support* really mean? I think good leadership looks like taking your team's side when the opportunity arises. If we don't treat our patients well, the business may go sideways and possibly close its doors. Support means giving my team all the tools and training they need to deliver an amazing experience to our patients.

On the other hand, we don't tolerate our patients treating our staff poorly. I will get on the phone and speak to that patient to explain that while we understand they were frustrated, our team consists of great people and the patient can't talk to or treat them poorly. We have zero tolerance for that. Good leaders will have their teams' backs.

We also create a culture of *everyone does everything*. We have cross-trained our entire team so if clinical staff is running behind on sterilization, the front-end team can help. If the phones are ringing off the hook, our hygienist can easily pick it up, as she has been trained in call conversion.

Accountability

This is a big one. You're not helping anybody if you're not holding them accountable, and you shoot yourself in the foot when you don't hold yourself accountable. You're just not doing any good. It starts with you. Good leaders hold people accountable. You live up to a well-defined value system. For example, you don't say you value good relationships with people and then hate talking to people.

Accountability also flows up the chain, as well. I feel that good leaders encourage their team to hold them accountable.

"A person's success in life can usually be measured by the number of uncomfortable conversations he or she is willing to have."
~Tim Ferris

Listening

Listening is probably the most important part of communicating, so it's in a category of its own. To me, listening goes much deeper than hearing spoken words. Listening includes *understanding* and *empathy*. Understanding means I am certain I received your message the way you intended, while empathy means I appreciate your position and have a high regard for your feelings.

In short, I work on listening, but that doesn't mean I necessarily agree with what I hear. It's only after I have listened that I can provide direction and mentorship or hold my team accountable. Listening is the anchor for all other leadership activities.

Give all the Credit, Take all the Blame.

As an entrepreneur, I also love to step in and solve problems. I love to help! This drives me to create ideas, systems or solutions that help get us past multiple obstacles in our day-to-day operations. I may be the "mastermind," but the members of my team are the executors. They learn, adhere to and consistently execute in order to ensure the solution works. When we overcome the hurdle and it's time to give credit, I give it to the team. I don't say,

> *"It's a good thing I created that protocol. It worked well!"*

Instead, I say,

> *"Thanks, team, for all of your hard work that helped us get past this hurdle. Great job!"*

No matter how significant my contribution, I always acknowledge the team's role and thank them for that. This level of humility and appreciation is what leadership is all about. I appreciate receiving credit for hard work as much as anyone. A little validation goes a long way. I just resist that temptation, because it feels equally as good to see how pleased my team is when they receive this level of approval and validation, as well.

On the other side, I am the one responsible for anything that goes wrong. I have the final authority on who is on our team, what the processes should be and what decisions we make. When it doesn't work, I am ALWAYS the one responsible. I embrace it. I have been doing this for years. The interesting thing is, my core team and those I work most closely with will typically say, *"No, it's not. It's my fault, or all of ours. You can't always take the blame for everything, Justin."*

This speaks volumes!

***

"If you want to go fast, go alone.
If you want to go far, go together."
`African Proverb

What I am about to tell you is contrary to most (if not all) the books you have read or speakers you follow on the subject of management and self-development and may be quite controversial.

YOU CAN DO IT ALL BY YOURSELF…

You can try to perform every task yourself or micro-manage everything your team needs to do. You know you can because you are a hard worker. You put yourself through dental school, and that was really hard. No one studied for you or wrote those exams for you. You did all of that on your own and were successful. I am telling you that you *can* build your practice by yourself.

BUT IT SUCKS!

You can micromanage everything if you want to, as long as you plan on being small and stressed. You can be a one-person operation if you want to work long hours, more than five days a week and rarely take a vacation. You can do it all yourself if you never want to grow your income or your nest egg. You can do it all yourself if you never want to achieve all the reasons you listed *WHY* you do what you do.

I promise I will always be honest with you. This is an honest moment. You need to master the art of delegation. Without working at improving this skill, you limit your ability to expand your operations and increase the size of your practice.

You're Not Good at Everything

When I was putting 60-80 hours a week into my practice while learning AND earning less every week, I had to be completely honest with myself. My first realization was that I can't continue this pace over my 40-year career.
When I stopped and had an honest conversation with myself and with the help of my wife, I realized I suck at a lot of things and other people should be doing that work.

You Don't Have the Time

Time is one thing every person on this planet has in common. We ALL have the same 24 hours in a day. Though some will have more days than others, it is true that once the day has passed, there is nothing you can do to get it back.

You get to choose how you spend your 24 hours every day. Spending your time on low-value tasks will rob you of your ability to make decisions and will increase suffering from decision fatigue and carry-over lag. Both of these are principles in neuroscience and psychology which are proven to significantly affect your judgment and productivity.

decision-fatigue

Noun
(*uncountable*)

- (psychology) The deteriorating quality of decisions made by an individual after a long session of decision making.

Dentists and small business owners who try to go it alone or micromanage everything suffer from decision fatigue. The quality of their decisions drops because they have so many to make, simple and complicated. Both Steve Jobs and Mark Zuckerberg have admitted in public that they choose to wear the same clothes every day, removing one more decision they need to make each day. Jobs wore his signature turtleneck and Zuckerberg his notable t-shirt.

Carryover lag, in its most simple form, explains that previous decisions have a residual effect on our current decisions as the emotional attachment carries over. Many of our day-to-day decisions have unnoticeable effects, as emotional attachment is low. For example, what you choose to eat for lunch. Other decisions, those with higher risk or that require more energy, can have an impact on your subsequent decisions for a number of days. The bigger the decision, the bigger the carry-over lag.

Learning Lesson

In his book Outliers, Malcom Gladwell professes that it takes ~10,000 hours of deliberate practice to master a skill or a subject. He uses the Beatles as an example and suggests all the nights spent playing in clubs and days practicing for gigs make them masters in their craft. You have also spent the time to become a master. In your time going to dental school and working in your practice, you may have spent more than 10,000 hours of deliberate practice in your profession. How much time do you think you have available to master skills like accounting/bookkeeping, reception or operations? That's a lot of hours! Mastering the art of delegation is building a team who are masters in their crafts and enabling them to get the work done.

Michael Gerber describes this as *working in your business versus on your business* in his book ***The E-Myth***. Mastering the art of delegation starts with just getting over the fact that nobody is going to do the work exactly the way you want it done. It's an unfortunate reality, but is acceptable, as long as you know the result you are looking for.

Even if the job is done 80% of the way you would like to see it, it will be good enough. An 8/10 for most of the work I need to delegate is pretty good. As a dentist, I take a lot of pride in my work, even to the point of being a perfectionist. That's what our clients deserve when we are working in their mouths. If, because I chased perfectionism, I insisted on doing the bookkeeping, answering the phones, following up on appointments, cleaning the treatment rooms, ordering supplies and so on, everything would suffer.

Another way to look at it is if I delegate a task to someone who can only do 50% of what I could do if I did it, then it is 50% more than I could have done by myself.

Rules for Delegating Effectively:

- Delegate high- and low-value tasks to the right people.
- Be okay with *good enough* for certain tasks.

- Have confidence in the person/people to whom you are delegating.
- Have the other person paraphrase what you want in their own words to confirm understanding.
- Set a deadline for completion and then follow up.

High- and low-value tasks that can be done by someone else should be. A good rule of thumb is if the task can be completed by someone else for between $10-$100 per hour, it should be delegated. This, of course, includes lawyers and accountants, although I suspect you will be unable to find one in that price range!

There are some tasks that you just have to be okay with *good enough*. Anything that does not directly affect the client can be good enough. For example, does the supplies closet need to be organized exactly the way you want it? Probably not. Does the lobby need to be clean and organized? Absolutely.

The most critical piece for delegation is that you need to have confidence in the people to whom you are delegating. They need to have the skill, ability and desire to be able to perform the delegated task or activity.

Next, request the person paraphrase back to you what needs to be accomplished in their own words. This will confirm understanding.

Lastly, set a deadline for completion and follow up to confirm the work was done. This may be at the end of day, the end of week or whatever timeline is appropriate. The structure sets an expectation.

There is little more that will destroy credibility and authority quicker than assigning a task and not following up for completion--especially if the task is not completed and there is no accountability after the fact.

Once you have all six elements, step back and get out of their way. If this person doesn't deliver, you may need to find another individual. If they are a team member and not a third party, first ask yourself if you have trained them adequately, or if you have assigned the wrong kind of task to this individual. Delegate knowledgeably and consistently. *What do you want them to do, how do you want them to do it, when do you want it done by and do they understand?* That has freed up a lot of time for me, and that's why I'm able to take this time and share it with you.

That is the difference between having a light touch (control) versus a heavy hand (insanity).

The Anchor of Delegation

Understanding *why* a task needs to be done a certain way is the anchor of mastering delegation. When the person to whom you are delegating understands why they need to do it, it increases the likelihood they will put forth a good effort and complete the task as requested.

For example: I was delegating the documentation of the in-office systems to two individuals--one clinical and one administrative. We had several discussions. One was about why this task was so important. I explained that it was important that we were very accurate in our documentation process because we wanted to be detailed in such a way that we could give this to a Grade 10 student, and they could come in and do that job. That's what we wanted. I asked if we were clear about what we wanted, and my delegates said okay. I explained further--this was important because it was going to reduce the time that we spent training people. It was going to reduce the frustration the office managers experienced. It was going to minimize mistakes and it was going to allow us to hold people accountable when they came on board. No longer would we have a receptionist say, "I didn't know I was supposed to do it like that," because now we had that accountability tool. The documentation would allow us to provide great service and live out our mission.

So now they understood why. If I wasn't thorough in my explanation, my delegates would question why they needed to do this six-month's worth of hard work. That is clear when you delegate.

***

A beautiful statement from Simon Sinek in his book ***Start with Why*** is,

> *"People don't buy what you do; they buy why you do it. And what you do simply proves what you believe."*

He is referring more to getting buy-in to a mission and vision. I have successfully implemented this concept in mastering the art of delegation, or simply getting stuff done. Here is his Golden Circle:

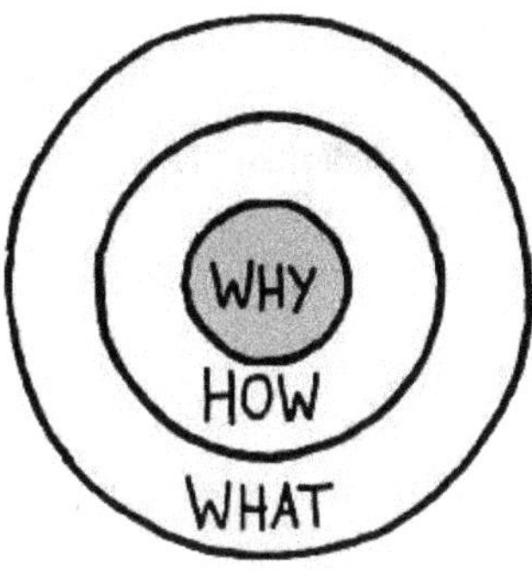

Starting at the center is a discussion of WHY. In other words, what is your purpose? When you explain the *why* of the task, you achieve a fundamental understanding of the true accomplishment needed. Remember the product of the product???? Same applies here. The *why* is the product of the product at the task level. If people understand why you're asking them to do a task, you increase the chances of getting the best work from them.

You will get their best work in the HOW, which is the process--the specific actions taken to realize the *why*.

These are the steps needed to generate some sort of result that demonstrates we have achieved the *why*.

Those results are the WHAT--the result of the *why,* or the proof.

Let's recap my example of delegation from earlier:

Why	Happy, Satisfied, Loyal Teammates
How	Implement a standard documentation process
What	o Reduce the time that we spend training people. o Reduce the frustration that the office managers have. o Minimize mistakes. o Hold people accountable when they come on board.

When they know the *why*, they know its importance. The results are not just incremental. They are exponential. I found that when I explained the WHY and we explored the HOW together, the WHAT achieved far more than what I expected. That's because I have empowered our people to do what they are good at. They often found solutions that were 100x better than I would have thought.

Exercise

TIME LOG: For one full week, write down everything you do in a given day. After one week, you'll be able to determine what you do and where your time is spent.

Ask yourself what you can immediately delegate and do that. This is the only way to free up the time you need to work on your business and focus on high-value tasks.

This entire chapter has been leading up to this: *influence.*

Here is my take on it. Influence is persuading people to do what YOU want for THEIR reasons.

It's a skill all leaders have to have. No one is going to follow you if you can't influence them. No one is buying from you if you can't influence them. No one is doing anything if you can't influence them. One way to become influential is to teach someone how to think.

This is an area in which I have been working hard to improve. I like to leverage the experts. Brendon Burchard describes his High-Performance Habit #5 as *Develop Influence.*

We need to:

- Teach people how to think (Train People)
- Challenge people to grow and contribute

In all of my practices, I find it extremely important that my team think about customer service with the same reverence as I do. I teach them.

I can easily describe the 10 attributes which are important in our customer service. But telling isn't teaching. Teaching is being a leader, not a boss. I teach my team to think

about customer service like inviting a guest into your home. How do you think you would treat that guest? This, in part, teaches my team to think about empathy.
When they think about experiences they have had where they spent some money and were feeling good, they start to think a certain way. Then they behave a certain way. In other words, I use my influence to persuade them to do something I want them to do and they do it for their reasons.

In other words, lead by example. When you want people to do things, show them how to do it. Do it yourself. Be consistent. That's how you'll influence them. Define what you want people to do and do it yourself. Just show them how. This is the lead-by-example piece of the puzzle and I think it is the most important. They will pick up on your energy.

I feel the need to clarify here. When I suggest that you show them how to do what you want them to do, consider the task. If you want your team to show up on time with a ton of energy, ready to deliver *wow* experiences, then that's what you need to do, day-in and day-out.

Perhaps you need them to follow steps in your bookkeeping or appointment follow-up systems. In this case, you need to provide a means to have your people trained as opposed to showing them yourself. But it's important that your team knows that they have your support.

Here is what may happen when you are not consistent. You could spend an entire year preaching about something in particular, like customer service, and you screw it up one time and lose all of your momentum. Your team starts to think, *See that? I told you it wasn't important.*

That's when I start to deflate. I think, *Seriously? I've been working my butt off and then it just fizzles out?*

At first, Influence may feel uncomfortable. You have to be strong, and that's okay. It's not your team's job to know this stuff. You're the leader. When I have a patient who's difficult or I'm afraid to talk to them about something and I back down, I'm going to lose that momentum with my team.

But there's an antidote to that. The antidote is to be vulnerable and say, "I'm not perfect guys. Tell me when I'm not living up to it. I'm not planning to fall off and I will work every day to be consistent."

Share how you're working hard on it. Share how nervous you may be to go into particular appointment with a patient. I sometimes am. But you know what? I have to tell myself, "Look. Go in there and get this done. This is *why* you have to do it."

Then *boom*! I get it done and I'm better for it. Sometimes I don't get it done and I need my team to point that out to me. I think that is the antidote and how you can minimize the risk of losing momentum. You're not perfect. You're teaching them to think and acknowledge that you're all working hard and possibly struggling. You're going to do your best to live into this every day. And you demonstrate that to them so when you do screw up, all the work you've done to this point isn't completely erased.

When you're consistent, you're teaching your team how to think. Consistency drives a positive result. Customer service equals happiness--not just for the patient, but for you and your team.

Ideas to Remember

- Who do I need to become?
- Leadership is about showing not telling.
- Be the example.
- Teach | Show | Explain instead of Tell | Show | Do
- Measure the results and hold people accountable.
- Give all the credit and take all the blame.
- You can do it all by yourself, but it sucks!
- Master the art of delegation.
- Explain the *why* in every task you want completed.
- Teach people how to think to become influential.

CHAPTER SEVEN

McDonald's x Google = High-Performance Practice

"Even if you're flippin' burgers at McDonald's, if you are excellent, everybody wants to be in your line."
~Oprah Winfrey

This chapter title probably sounds really funny at first read. What do we really have to learn about building a high-performance practice from McDonald's? They don't exactly make the best burger in the world. Some may even argue they don't even make a *good* hamburger. But as Oprah suggests, "... if you are excellent, everybody wants to be in your line."

I hope it's obvious that we're not about to discuss making burgers or delivering cheap and efficient service. If you have ever read about the McDonald brothers or watched a documentary about their story (there is a really interesting movie called 'The Founder' which tells a different part of the McDonald's story), you know that the brothers were very good at logically and sequentially organizing steps into a process which could be duplicated with predictable results.

The system they built could deliver the same quality product every time AND they could train anyone to do it. Look at how well it has worked! I have been hard-pressed to find any other example of a multi-national, multi-billion-dollar enterprise that could be run by teenagers.

But we are not teenagers and we are not delivering the same cheeseburger a thousand times per day. We are doctors. What could we possibly have in common with a McDonald's franchise? Nothing, really...on the surface.

What did a hamburger shack like McDonald's in the 1930's have in common with an automobile manufacturer like Ford? Nothing, until Richard and Maurice McDonald implemented an assembly-line method for selling hamburgers where the quality control measures were as tight as the Ford Model 74 of the time.

What about Google? What does a billion-dollar tech company have to do with your dental office? The same thing every business has in common--*people*! They recruit and retain A-players and give them the freedom to implement creative solutions. They are flexible versus rigid and encourage out-of-the-box thinking. This empowerment and support increases engagement and produces more desirable outcomes.

I am not an advocate for rigid systemization, nor am I all for pure flexibility. The hybrid between the two is what I believe works best in a service-based industry. Recruit, train and retain A-players. This is part systemization and training (non-negotiable) and part empowerment and ownership (flexibility and encouragement of creativity/best judgement).

Systemization

In our service-based businesses (remember I use business interchangeably with practice), we need to build systems to create consensus. Think back to Chapter Four in ROI-based marketing where we talked a lot about systems. In order to manage your marketing ROI, you have to have a system to generate leads and close them into clients. You need to track, measure, adjust and re-deploy.

That's only one-half of the discussion. The other half is about retention, and that means value. Retention requires creating great experiences and educating people. That requires systems to:

~Generate leads
~Nurture and convert
~Retain your clients

More than that, why wouldn't you want your clients to become raving fans? These are the patients who insist all their friends and family see you, too. What do you think an advocate's ROI is? I can tell you that it is through the roof!

It doesn't just happen, however. Great experiences and raving fans don't arise from a business by default (See Chapter Four and Chapter Nine). Your practice must become a business by design. Your practice requires systems.

A Tale of Two Doctors

Dr. B. was an intelligent and hardworking man. He came from the humble beginnings of a working-class family. Dr. B always had a strong desire to be successful and make his family proud, so he chose to enter into dentistry. He had considered becoming a lawyer or M.D., but neither appealed to his ambitious nature nearly as much as dentistry. For the same time spent, he knew he could be a great dentist AND build an amazing business compared to that of other professions. So, as Dr. B. completed dental school and started working as a professional, he worked up to the level of his ambition. Dr. B. wasn't afraid to put in the time to get it done. He worked incredibly long days and had little time to himself.

Dr. J. (not the basketball player) was also an intelligent and hardworking dentist. He was an ambitious young dentist who wanted a lot for himself and his family. He aspired to achieve success and also wanted to enjoy the journey along the way.

Dr. J. studied more than just medical/dental books and whitepapers. He invested a ton of money to work on his own development. Even though he was quite shy growing up, he wasn't shy about learning.

He attended every seminar he could afford the time to attend. Dr. J. invested time and money in masterminds, coaching and engaging with other successful people. That's how he learned he must build his practice using systems, leadership, and creating a great culture. He started working on his marketing systems. He felt awkward at first because he was a dentist and not a marketer, but he soon found people he could rely on to help him. As his practice grew, he was able to attract a lot of great people to his team and together, they built systems for operations, training, accounting and customer service.

Dr. J was happy he was able to have a positive impact in his patients' and team members' lives and was grateful he could afford to spend quality time with his family on his own terms.

I was both doctors. I was Dr. B when I started my career. Full of energy, ambition, confidence and ignorance. I was working my butt off and found that while I was making good money, I was working harder and harder to earn it. I had done well in getting patients in the door, converting them to treatment and making raving fans out of them. I chose to expand, and with expansion comes magnification of both the good and the bad. The issue was, I didn't have as many well-defined and documented systems as I should have, and this led to major stress, weight gain, strain on my relationships and scaling issues. The worst part is that I wasn't enjoying the way I was building my practice.

I became Dr. J when I began confiding in other successful doctors and entrepreneurs across many industries. I attended every seminar I could to meet successful people and glean how they'd become that way. I learned many things. One of the most important lessons I learned was how to build systems. By now you should notice a theme here. I didn't become successful by accident. I didn't become successful because I was smart. I became successful because I was willing to fail, learn and quickly move on, but I also knew success leaves clues. I understood that there were others ahead of me and they had the answers I needed. So, I sought them out. I didn't talk, but rather listened to what they had to say, which enabled me to gather tremendous information to use in my own practice to produce the same outcomes.

The bottom line is that there are no new problems. Someone has figured it out before you. Just find them. Fortunately for you, I have made so many mistakes that I can help you with most problems, and if I can't, I definitely know where to go to help you find the answers.

Build a System that Runs Your Business.
Then just Run the System.

Your practice is not a system if it does not achieve:

- Replication
- Scale

Replication

A system is something you can replicate. Here are some simple questions you can ask to test the quality of your system:

- Can we teach a reasonable person to do the tasks and generate the same result?
- If we were to lose a key employee for a time, could we fill the position without a loss in the quality of our service?
- Do we get the same results every time we perform the tasks at hand?
- How easily can we correct a mistake?

Your system is not repeatable if you cannot teach and perform the tasks to be completed and achieve the same results consistently.

Scalable

Scale is another critical component of a well-designed system. Scale, in the context of a high-performance practice, means that:

- An additional unit of input produces a multiple of output (e.g. 8-10x).
- The output increase is predictable.

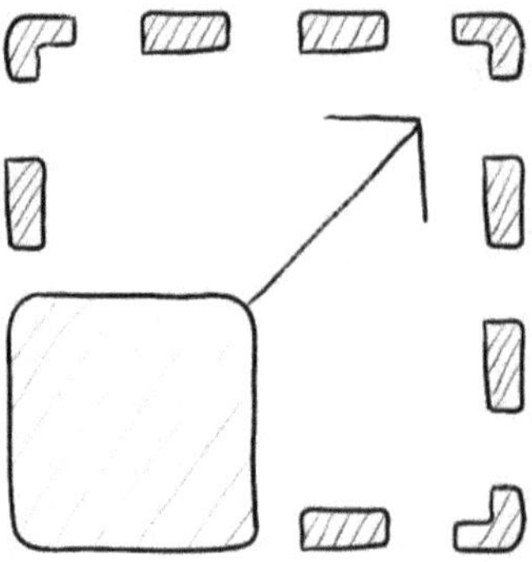

In other words, you should get back more than what you put in (time, money, fulfillment, etc.). You should also be able to forecast, with accuracy, how much you will get back when you put more in (time, money).

Now you see how much in common your practice has with an organization like McDonald's. Who is more repeatable and scalable than McDonald's? Nobody (well maybe Starbucks, but you get the point). Do we have something to learn and apply there? Absolutely.

***

Here is a little-known secret--a high-performance practice is quite boring to operate. It's truly not the least bit exciting. This is a little tongue in cheek, of course, but the meaning behind it is that a successful practice run by systems doesn't contain a lot of volatility.

It's the volatility that creates dramatic spikes and dips because of all the emergencies needing to be handled day-in and day-out. When you have built your high-performance practice by design rather than operating it by default, you will find the number of fires you must put out in a day reduces significantly. I am not saying it's bliss, it's just much easier. After all, you're in business, and as CEO, you will always have issues with which to deal, high-performance practice or not. The goal is to get to a point where you are focusing on high-level problems vs. low-level tasks like approving holiday schedules or having to decide whether an associate doctor can order a new type of local anesthetic.

There is one thing I need you to understand as you start to feel the weight of implementing systems, policies and procedures pressing down on your shoulders. The goal is improvement and not perfection. You will absolutely bury yourself if you attempt to implement everything at once and with immense detail.

Photo: seangallo.com

Have you ever heard of the best way to eat an elephant? You guessed it. One bite at a time. The system you are going to build that will run your high-performance practice is an elephant and will need to be built one piece at a time.

The simplest way to start to build your system is to start by giving everyone on your team a sheet of paper and have them write down exactly what they're doing. This will require some tact (remember the discussion of influence in the last chapter) if you have never asked this question before. Your staff may feel somewhat threatened, as if their quality of work is being questioned. It's not, and it will be important to help them understand that (see section about explain the why of every task in Chapter Five).
One way to position the reason you are asking is:

"We will use these sheets to train other people when they join the team. As you know, it has been very challenging to train new teammates and we all feel the stress of that. If you write down exactly how you complete your tasks every 20 minutes for the rest of the day, we can start to put this together."

You will end up with a list of the roles and responsibilities for each person on shift that day. You can do the same with the shift on duty the next day, or the same shift, if they are doing different tasks. That will be the start of your onboarding/operations manual. This should set off a couple of light bulbs for you, because Chapter Three was all about management and measurement. The same applies here. You can't measure or manage a process that is not clearly defined and written down.

Now the true beauty in this is that you and your team can continue to rework those steps. Tweak them as you go so they get better and better. YOU can decide what is important to improve first. YOU get to choose where the team spends their focus.

For my dollar, the first place I spend my attention is in cost reduction.

The only way to make profit is to sell more, spend less or both at the same time. Selling more takes time and influence. You have 100% control over your expenses today. Your practice is leaking cash through overhead and other

SG&A (Selling, General and Administrative) expenses. This is the lowest-hanging fruit that will yield quick results with just a little bit of attention.

A high-performance practice will use a very simple tool as a system to manage expenses: the budget. Remember that a business cannot survive long without cash flow. Mismanaging expenses will quickly result in business failure.

The five major cost centers that will require most of your attention are:

- Rent [5% or less]
- Wages [25%-30% or less] (includes all wages/salaries, payroll taxes and fees, and benefits)
- Lab [9% or less] (crown/bridge lab, removable prosthetics, implant and ortho lab) *
- Dental supplies: [5% or less] (general dental supplies and ortho supplies) **
- Office supplies

*Some offices choose to place cerec blocks, ortho/implant brackets/fixtures/lab under supplies. If this is your preference, keep it consistent and understand that these percentages will change. Alternative reporting: supplies + lab = 14% or less combined.

**All numbers above are a percentage of adjusted production. You can also report them as a percentage of collections, in which case they will relatively increase (if your collections are less than 100% of your adjusted production). In my practices we choose to report them as a percentage of adjusted production.

***Regional variances may apply.

Step One in reducing your costs is to allocate a budget for all the expense line-items in your Profit & Loss Statement (P&L). Step Two is to monitor those figures, reviewing them regularly. How regularly? It depends on how much you're spending in those line items and how often they change. The higher the figures, the more detailed a review is needed. The higher the number of transactions, the more often you should review them. At an absolute minimum, your budget should be reviewed once per month.

Some of these line items you may have more influence over month-to-month than others. Rent, for example, can only be negotiated at the beginning of a lease period (occasionally mid-lease, but that is rare) so the figure is less critical to watch short-term.

Wages are more subjective and worthy of constant attention. Cutting wages to save on expenses can have a negative impact on your practice. Team members who feel they are not being fairly and equitably compensated deliver results which reflect that belief, and service quality can begin to suffer. It can also reduce the chances of your ability to recruit A-players. In our practices, we choose to compensate our team members well. Therefore, our wages are at the top end of the spectrum locally. Why? Because we want to attract, train and retain the best and eliminate A-players from jumping ship due to minor wage increases offered by competitors. (There are obviously limits to this and each position has a cap regardless of what competitors are offering. In addition, not everyone gets a raise just because 365 days has elapsed since their last one.) Lastly, it is important to note that you have a choice to pay by the hour or salary. There are pros and cons to each method.

A note about the irrational fear of dentists. "My patients and team will leave me if…." Let's focus on the team part for a second…your team will leave you if you have poor leadership, office culture, attitude and compensation. However, compensation becomes less relevant when you focus on the other three areas. Let me explain. It is unlikely your staff will leave you for an extra dollar-per-hour if you take a genuine interest in them, empower them to be the best at what they do through training and express sincere appreciation for everything they do for the practice and the patients. In the absence of this, you will definitely see higher turnover regardless of compensation.

So how do you compensate your team members fairly and equitably while trying to budget? Think about it in terms of return on activity (ROA). For example: A hygienist should be billing a minimum of 3.3 times their wages. You can also calculate this to the team as a whole. The office should be producing approximately 25-30K per fulltime team member (regional variances will apply). This allows you to determine if you are overstaffed. In the event you are overstaffed, consider cutting back and simply increasing the salary/wages of one of your A-players.

Your lab expenses can be negotiated as your practice grows. The more lab services you require, the better you will be able to negotiate for volume discounts.

Expenses for sundries and consumables can be managed through negotiation or control of their use. You may be able to negotiate pricing with suppliers. A larger cash leak often finds its way into your practice through waste. Effective use of your sundries should be monitored by the numbers.

You have got to know your numbers. The figures are the evidence that your system is either working or is broken. Your numbers also show you where you need to focus. The systems you implement to run your operations are what you use to survive, stabilize and thrive in your practice.

The next important step for systemization is:

New Patient Experience

Think about this process from the moment your marketing has hit the mark and a new patient wants to engage with you. Your system needs to be able to address some high-level questions:

- How do we answer the phone?

- How do we greet them when they arrive?
- What do our forms look like?
- How do we invite them into the chair?
- How do we communicate with them?
- Do we build relationships and record the information we learn about them?

Once you have all of the steps laid out in front of you and your team can execute those steps consistently, then you've got to get into the nitty-gritty. This is the testing and retesting process so you can optimize (a nice buzzword businesspeople like to use to mean *improve*). This is not unlike the scientific process you're used to.

THE SCIENTIFIC METHOD

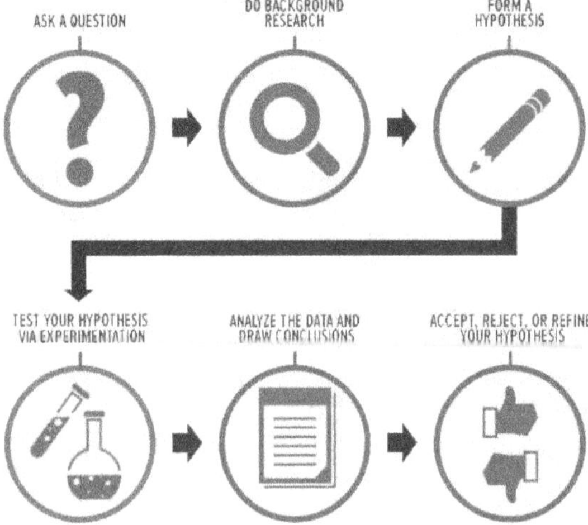

Developing and testing your systems, policies and procedures looks A LOT like this. Now that you have a number of steps organized in a process, you can ask the question, *what part is not working?*. Then you can research by asking your team and your clients what could be improved. Next, you form a hypothesis, for example changing a hypothetical Step C. Then you change Step C and monitor the results. Continue to change Step C until you have the result you want. Then accept and implement the change. Lastly, use the same method to refine all of your processes. This method is called *Continuous Improvement* or CI, if you ask a business school graduate.

Running your high-performance practice is simply executing all the steps required to attract patients, fulfill the service and retain your clients. It is simple but not easy. There can be thousands of steps required to operate your practice. That is why I want you to remember you can only eat an elephant one bite at a time. If you adopt the mindset of *improvement* and not *perfection*, you will be well on your way to a high-performance practice.

The FOUR Core Systems include new client acquisition, cashflow management, patient/client retention, and team development and training.

Client Retention

- *Reappointment* – This is a component of client retention. It includes tracking who did not book appointments, when they need to be contacted and other steps in nurturing your patients to ensure they book their next appointment.

- *New-Patient Experience* (including treatment presentation protocol)
- *Customer Service Protocols/wow Experiences*
- *Painless, Efficient and Durable Dentistry*
- *Reactivation* - Reaching out to patients who have not been in the office for 18 months or longer. Attrition should be monitored regularly, and lists maintained.

New Client Acquisition

- *Internal Marketing* - What forms do you use? How do they look? What materials do you provide patients? This also includes patient onboarding, presentation of available services, target marketing to your active patient base and referral generation from the existing patient base.
- *External Marketing* – Strategic positioning (authority status), how all of your digital assets are developed and used (web site, social media, etc.), advertising (on-line and offline), media, collateral (brochures, sell sheets, etc.), events and trade shows, lead generation and Google review strategy, to name a few.

****Everything you do is marketing. All touch points matter! You must begin to think of yourself as a marketing agency that provides dental services.****

Cash Flow Management

- *Overhead Control*
- *Accounts Receivable and Collections* - Collecting copays from patients, cheque entry, insurance reimbursement negotiations and embezzlement protection

Professional Development and Training

- *Onboarding New Staff*
- *Ongoing Training*
- *Continuing Education*
- *Bimonthly Performance Evaluations*

This was really difficult for me when I decided I wanted to build a high-performance practice, so I can appreciate how daunting this might feel for you. The good news is that you don't have to do it all at once. In fact, I am suggesting that you don't. You would be absolutely normal if you also felt that all this management will be overwhelming. The good news is there are lots of software tools that can manage and even automate much of this for you.

The work for you and your team will be in understanding your practice--how each of you work within it to fulfill your service promise to your patients and then living up to it. The software is only as good as the people using it.

There are tools to manage your marketing efforts. Some require a little bit of effort while others are as simple as a push of a button. There are also highly trained and qualified advisers who can do this for you. There are accounting tools and patient-tracking platforms that can provide you more information about your practice than you can probably use, all of which can be very effective when you have implemented strong systems, policies and procedures.

***

You and your team have done a ton of work building systems, policies and procedures but you're still failing! Did you clearly define everyone's role and the responsibilities they need to fulfill?

Ahhhhh...that's the missing piece here. It's great that you have a well-designed system and you've mapped out what tasks need to be done in what order. The other half of the equation is to clearly outline who is responsible for which pieces.

I explained earlier in this chapter that we start this process by having each person write down everything they do on a daily basis. This helped us understand the work each team member was doing and identify any gaps in what we felt they should be doing.

The obvious note here is that the person who made a particular list of activities should be the person responsible to carry them out. That's simple enough. If the job is *receptionist*, the list belongs to the person who performs those duties.

There are two other roles I would like you to think about. Who is responsible for overseeing that these tasks are completed as written?
What other roles are needed to ensure tasks can be completed?

Let's go back to our receptionist. Who is responsible to ensure the reception tasks are completed as written? For the most part, it would be the person who supervises the receptionist, such as the office manager.

What other roles are needed to ensure the reception tasks can be completed? The receptionist will most definitely need the tools to do the job, like phones, a computer, software and training. Sometimes these seem obvious, but it can be tricky when looking at other roles in your system.

That's the power of an effective system! Part of a well-defined role of the receptionist position is who is responsible for overseeing that position and what they need to do.

***** *WARNING* *****

You may tend to be too specific in defining the steps, tasks and roles, or have unrealistic expectations on the completion of this tasks. This is an opportunity for you to learn from one of my many mistakes. When I first clued into what it was going to take to build the high-performance practice I wanted to have, I read ***The e-Myth*** written by Michael Gerber (highly recommended). I read the chapter about systems and thought to myself, YES!
So, I jumped on it and sent an email to four of my team members on a Friday. In it, I said:

> *"Team, we're going to have a meeting on Monday morning to discuss documentation of all in-office systems to build a step-by-step system. This is going to serve as the platform for us to have turnkey operations, including onboarding, with ongoing training for our team members. This meeting will be two hours. By the end, I'd like to have a comprehensive system list, with the goal of creating a final copy of our operations manual in the next three months."*

No one replied to the email.

The three lessons here:

- Your system can be over engineered, and the scope can be too large for what you really need.
- You're not trying to build robots and have every minute of every day precisely laid out.
- Understand that this takes time. It's a process.

Start with only the most important parts of your system, which will make implementation easier and faster. Decide on which parts are non-negotiable and then be flexible with everything else.

Think about five or six inflexible key systems. Let your team know they have the freedom to operate as they see fit. For example, if your software allows for five different ways to enter a new patient, let them enter it the way they like, as long as the result is the same.

This is an important part of defining everyone's role. You have a talented team. Leave them room within your system to use their skills and knowledge to amplify the benefits of your system. You will thank me for it later.

***

Believe it or not, mapping out your processes and building your systems is the easier part of building a high-performing practice. The most difficult piece is ensuring everyone on your team is crystal-clear on their tasks. No matter how much you feel you have explained, there is always room for interpretation.

Being clear about the non-negotiable tasks (which must be done in a certain way) and flexible about everything else will serve you AND your team well. To do so, the high-performing practice must collaborate as a team.

More coming on building your dream team in the next chapter.

Team collaboration will mold your system into a malleable and working system where everyone has a defined role and is clear on their tasks. There's a values system here and all the team members help each other with clarity.

You can't watch how and when everyone performs every one of their tasks. That's not leadership. It isn't teaching. It isn't delegation. All you can do is monitor your numbers. Perhaps you are getting a 98% positive feedback rating from patients, which indicates customer service and experience is good. It wouldn't make sense for you to go up to your receptionist and critique the one phone call you thought they didn't answer the way you wanted.

Coming full circle back to *Chapter Three: You Can't Manage What You Can't Measure*, the results will point out what needs to be fixed. Perhaps it is the receptionist who is converting 50% of new patient leads/calls into patient exams or appointments. The numbers indicate there is a problem and the fix is to train. Even better, have one of your staff who is getting 90% call conversion work with your receptionist to help them improve.

That's the power of a system! At the end of the day, I care more about predictable, repeatable and scalable results. If one person is slightly different than another but gets the same results, who cares? *Results* count. The bottom line is to train your team on the system, empower them to use their best judgment, avoid micromanagement, track their results (lag indicators), hold them accountable and repeat training as needed.

***

I have used a lot of buzzwords, like systems, roles, responsibilities and so on. I understand they can be overused and lose their meaning. In the context of building a high-performance practice, my point is that you will need to know what results you want and figure out what your team needs to do day-in and day-out to achieve those results.

To keep this super simple, I'll outline the steps you need to follow to start documenting your system:

Discovery Meeting
Schedule a meeting with a key team member--your manager, or maybe it's your spouse--to discuss exactly what you're wanting to do (including WHY). Explain that you want to document all systems and processes in the office. You would like the information in a detailed and simple form so that it includes the step-by-step of each position, along with a flow chart if applicable and accountability tools (how you are going to measure the result of this process). Explain that you would like this done for each position and system. What you should have at the end is the start of a standard operations manual.

Task List

Now the key team member's job is going to be reaching out to the individual team members. They will meet with the receptionist, clinical assistant(s), hygienist(s) and dentist(s) and ask them to please list everything they do all day long. The result will be a relatively accurate *roles and responsibilities* list. Each of these roles, like checking patients in or out, converting patients into treatment plans or delivering treatments are tasks involved in new patient experience.

You are looking for enough detail that you get a good understanding of what your team actually does (not necessarily what it should be doing), but not so much detail that they document their mouse clicks on an intake form. I don't need to know everything about how a new patient is entered into the software, as long as we have all five pieces of necessary information.

Name, contact information (email, phone number), insurance breakdown/policy number and how they heard about the office. The order in which this information is collected is not important, nor is the EXACT verbiage. As long as they are polite and effective, leave them alone. Nit picking will only result in conflict and your team feeling you don't trust them to use their best judgment

Have the key team member review and add any items that were missed or overlooked and then get it reviewed for approval.

Identify Gaps

Decide what you are looking to accomplish. Write down all of the goals you have for your new high-performance practice. What do you want to see in terms of revenue, profit, new patients, treatment acceptance and many others? This is the purpose of your budget. Review all of the responsibilities lists your team has submitted with your key team member(s) or A-players.

> *Are these processes sufficient to get you where you plan to go?*
>
> *What things do you have to add?*
>
> *Are you missing systems?*
>
> *Are you missing components of systems?*
>
> *What are the right measurements to use to verify these processes are working?*

Brainstorm these with your key members. Then add those in. Now you have a workable model.

Draft Procedure

By this time, you probably have a lot of different versions and the documentation process is nearly complete. Use a clean sheet of paper and neatly rewrite (type!) the procedures. Include any supplementals like diagrams, measurements and references.

Review and Revise

Have your key team member(s) read and review each procedure to ensure continuity and suitability. If you do not have A-players as key members, find a mentor, a coach or another successful dentist. They may provide you with their system which you can then adapt to your needs. By the end of this step, you will have documented what you are doing now, made changes or added steps and are now ready to roll out your system.

Implement

Time to bring it to the people. Have a launch party! Celebrate this major milestone in your practice. Everyone should feel like this is a big win for them. Train each of your team members on the procedures for which they are responsible, along with how to provide feedback about what works and what doesn't throughout the coming weeks or months.

Measure

Measure your team's performance in each of those areas. Let's use accounts receivable (A/R) as an example. If your A/R system is good, you should be at 97% or more. Suppose you are continuously operating at 90%. There's no fraud and people are doing what you've asked them to do. The numbers indicate that there is a problem with the system, and it needs to be revisited. You can't manage what you can't measure.

Follow-Up

Measure the procedure and then go back to change the system or tweak it based on two things:

- *Metrics*
- *Staff and Patient Feedback*

Now is the time to ask questions. You may not be seeing results because the system doesn't work, although I have found it's more likely that the system is too complicated, or the team doesn't want to do it. That's why you have to get the team's feedback. That's number one. Why is this not working? Maybe it's too complicated. Maybe it's not clear.

Measurement is a tool which allows you to objectively evaluate the performance of any individual system, marketing modality or team member. The numbers don't tell the whole story. They are the clues to you that there is a story to be told about your high-performance practice.

For example, If I asked patients to rate Dr. Smith's personality on a scale from 1-10, I wouldn't get the whole story. If I knew Dr. Smith's treatment acceptance rate was only 60%, I could surmise that there may be a communication or relationship issue.

The mistake I see so many practices make is that they assume the treatment acceptance rates are low because the patients just didn't want to do treatment. That's far from the real story. The low number tells you a lot of other things. It indicates you have to fix communication. Your team is lacking in delivering the patient experience you want. All the low rate is doing is telling you where to focus your attention. Is it patient experience, customer service, quality of communication, conversion strategy/sales or flexible payment plans that require your attention--or is it something else?

Where you're winning. Where you're losing. Where to focus attention. I like that.

***

After you have worked so hard to build all these solid systems, implemented great policies and your procedures are ready to go, I am going to ask you to hold back a bit. I know, it's kind of like trying to get the racehorses back in the gates after the starter pistol has gone off.

"I would like you to be more self-reliant, show more initiative, and take greater personal responsibility — but check with me first!"

You may find you have the temptation to micromanage the entire system. Or at least parts of it. If you think you're immune, think again. Harry Chambers references a study by Trinity Solutions in his book My Way or the Highway which observed that 79% of respondents have experienced micromanagement. More than 2/3 (69%) of them considered changing jobs, while about 1/3 (36%) acted and left their positions.[ix]

Can you imagine all the time and money invested into building the systems for your high-performance practice just to be undone because you have trouble letting go?

Jack Wallen at *Pluralsight* listed the six dangers of micromanagement:[x]

- Loss of control
- Loss of trust
- Dependent employees
- Your own burnout
- High turnover of staff
- Lack of autonomy

Do you find it surprising that micromanagement results in loss of control instead of strengthening it? Wallen explains that micromanagement actual limits the management tools at your disposal, which also limits communication and eventually, your ability to manage.

So, here are three ways to measure whether you are micromanaging as a dentist:

How many times a day does your team ask you questions about how they should fulfill a role they should be performing on their own? How many questions do you get that you shouldn't have to answer?

How anxious are you when you delegate a task or allow your team to carry out their day-to-day duties? Do you step in often or do you allow them to carry out their tasks independently?

How many things are you doing today that you didn't expect or that you should not be doing as a dentist? Are you approving vacation and holiday schedules? Are you monitoring inventory and placing orders for supplies? Are you going through last week's schedule to determine who was booked or not? Are you having to discuss copayment or insurance issues daily?

If you were nodding your head as you were reading this, start delegating and train your people to do all these activities that occupy your time and energy and drain your focus. Your focus needs to shift to the things that are most important:

- Attracting the right people
- Training and retaining them
- Lowering costs
- Increasing case conversion
- Doing dentistry (What a notion! A dentist in the chair.)
- Getting patients in the door and keeping them
- Collecting money

These are the things the doctor should be looking at on a monthly or weekly basis so they can hold their team members accountable for the results. I am not suggesting that you must design a marketing campaign. Just that you should know which marketing strategies brought your patients in. You should know how many patients you lost the last month so you can hold yourself and your team accountable. Your job is leadership and accountability. The rest is just doing dentistry.

WHAT MICROMANAGERS REALLY MEAN WHEN THEY TRY TO EXPLAIN THEIR BEHAVIOR
Don't take the excuses at face value.

WHAT CHRONIC MICROMANAGERS SAY	WHAT THEY REALLY MEAN
It will save me time if I just do it myself.	*I don't believe it's worth my time to let them try, because they won't get it right anyway.*
Too much is at stake to allow this to go wrong.	*I don't trust them to do their jobs according to my standards.*
It's my credibility on the line if we don't get it done on time.	*The work won't get done unless I constantly prod them.*
When I am not involved, they mess up.	*The one time I yielded some control, there was a mistake and I'm not willing to take that risk again.*
My boss wants me to be heavily involved in my team's work.	*If I don't stay involved, how else will I prove my worth?*

SOURCE MURIEL MAIGNAN WILKINS, CO-AUTHOR OF *OWN THE ROOM: DISCOVER YOUR SIGNATURE VOICE TO MASTER YOUR LEADERSHIP PRESENCE* HBR.ORG

I love this little excerpt from Wilkins at the Harvard Business Review,[xi] describing signs that you are a micro manager. When I look back at different times in my career, I can honestly say that I have said (or thought) them all at least once, in one form or another. That's okay. What's not okay is to keep saying (or doing) these things. Not if you want to have a great team. Not if you want to build a high-performance practice.

***

The best place to start is at the beginning. McDonald's was founded on April 15, 1955. That was the first franchise.

Few people know that the restaurant was actually started in 1940. The McDonald brothers designed, tested, retested and refined their system for 15 years prior to Ray Kroc opening the first franchise and starting the global operation.

They originally started as a BBQ restaurant with 25 menu items. It was doing okay for the time. Then the brothers closed and reopened, dropping the menu down to three items--hamburgers, milkshakes and fries. Even the mighty McDonald's franchise had to retool their business.

What they decided to build when they reopened was a foundation. They kept the business simple, working on the most important pieces first. The system they built for delivering hamburgers formed the foundation for everything they do, even today. What they didn't do was move on to Step Two until Step One was solid.

You wouldn't want your builder to move on to framing your new mansion when the concrete foundation had not finished setting. The same applies to high-performance practices. You need to know your business. Go deep and get really good at one foundational item. Then go wide.

If you don't know what a receptionist should be doing, how they should be doing it and how to measure that result (e.g. conversion of new patients and call answer rate), then you shouldn't really be moving on to Step Two. If you're looking to open or acquire multiple practices, ensure that your first practice is finely tuned. Otherwise, you will be duplicating a poorly executed system, magnifying your problems and increasing your stress.

> *"Only a fool learns from his own mistakes. The wise man learns from the mistakes of others."*
> *~Otto von Bismarck*

I hope to save time, money and effort on your journey to building a high-performance practice. Business failure and cashflow emergencies can teach a cruel lesson, one I've experienced. This is a lesson you can learn through this book instead of experiencing it yourself.

Ideas to Remember

- Your high-performance practice will need well developed systems, policies and procedures.
- A good system is duplicatable and scalable.
- Know your numbers, as they are the indicators of success or a problem.
- Closely monitor your P&L.
- Everyone needs well-defined roles to fulfill.
- Be PATIENT. Systems take time to develop.
- Know which steps and systems are non-negotiable and which are flexible in the manner in which they are completed.
- Everyone on the team should be crystal clear on their tasks.
- Use your metrics and feedback to make adjustments.
- Do not micromanage.
- Document all systems.
- Your role as a leader is to hold people accountable to the systems.
- Identify the story behind the numbers. Are they a symptom of a problem?
- Build on a strong foundation first, then move onto the next step.

CHAPTER EIGHT

Build Your Dream Team

"Surround yourself with the best people you can find, delegate authority and don't interfere as long as the policy you've decided upon is being carried out."
~Ronald Reagan

Politics aside, Ronald Reagan sums up the last few chapters in one sentence. My interpretation is to find some awesome people to work with, set them up for success and then get out of their way. It just comes down to what are you looking to do? What does your high-performance practice look like to you? What is your *why*? If you're looking to grow a multi-million-dollar practice or business, you're not going to be able to do it alone. If want to have a profitable cashflow practice and take more time off for vacationing with your family, you're not going to be able to do it alone. You will need to surround yourself with people who are talented in certain areas.

I had a chance to receive mentorship from Kevin Harrington. If you don't know who Kevin Harrington is, make sure you Google him. He was one of the first to create successful infomercials and eventually launched the *As Seen on TV* brand. He said,

> *"I was strong-headed in the beginning and I wanted to do it all myself. Then I realized you've got to put together your dream team."*

You're not good at everything, nor should you be. It's better to get the right talent on the bus to begin with so you can actually grow, as opposed to spreading yourself too thin and being ineffective in delivering great results. You'll be miserable if you have to work on jobs you are not good at and don't like doing. If you have too much to do, even the jobs you enjoy lose their fulfillment. The teamwork makes the dream work.

Bottom Line: If you want to have the best business hire the best people!

Hire for Attitude and Train for Results

The one thing I have learned about personality traits is that you cannot teach a person how to like other people. It's not for a lack of trying, but naturally liking other people is just something that cannot be taught. That's huge. Healthcare is all about relationships, and if your team members don't understand people and how to develop relationships, your practice is doomed to fail.

My practice really started to grow shortly after I figured this out. I figured out that I needed to focus on the quality traits required for each position. Does a prospective team member connect with people? Do they enjoy interacting with other people and take a genuine interest in others? That's where we started to build our dream team. You are off to a good start if you can find a team who likes people, has good energy and is open to learning. There is a very good chance you will be able to train and mentor those people.

However, if anyone in your staff doesn't like people or is closed-minded to learning, you will have a lot of difficulty with that team member and will probably feel like you are banging your head against the wall.

We have a system when it comes to finding the people with the qualities and traits we're looking for.

How we pick our Dream Team

Step 1 Application	Step 2 Onboarding	Step 3 Maintenance
• Kolbe Survey • Phone Interview • Working Interview • Team Decision • Lunch Interview	• Office Tour • Employment Paperwork • Office Culture • Training	• Continued Training • Reviews • Monitor Results

The first step is the application. To complete the entire application process, a candidate for any position on our team must complete a Kolbe Survey. In short, the Kolbe Wisdom (http://www.kolbe.com/) suggests that instincts drive a person's behavior and that these behaviors lead to a pattern of an individual's unique method of operation or modus operandi (M.O.). We use the Kolbe assessments as a screening tool, as well as a guidance device, to determine the likelihood that we will have a good match of the individual's qualities and traits and the positions/roles we need to fill. We also use NY Times Bestselling Author, Gretchen Rubin's Four Tendencies quiz as a tool to determine how the team member (or potential team member) deals with inner and outer expectations. (Google: Gretchen Rubin Four Tendencies Quiz)

The next step is our list of prospective candidates we've selected to participate in a telephone interview with my office manager. They are amazing at establishing rapport quickly and getting the other person to feel comfortable enough to let their guard down and have a real conversation. There are specific steps the manager follows in this call, which includes a series of questions, along with sharing our mission, vision and values. There is a specific Kolbe score that can be used to increase the likelihood of matching the person to the correct role.

The third step is the working interview. I love this part of recruiting. We invite the candidate to come into our office and spend some time with the team during a normal workday. This serves both sides and helps all of us to get to know each other--the team and the prospective recruit. We also get to see how they might function in our professional environment. The length of the shift varies. All that matters is that the shift is long enough for the prospect to briefly shadow their potential position and for us to observe them.

The fourth step is that the team decides with the office manager whom they would like to hire. It makes sense, doesn't it? The team should have input into who they are going to spend the better part of their days working with side-by- side. This has had a profound impact in our camaraderie. The team feels they are part of the decision process and have ownership of the final decision. When the new recruit is hired, the entire team has a vested interest in helping them succeed. Oh, and the cherry on top of the recruitment sundae is that the new recruit KNOWS they were chosen by the team and now has ownership to live up to the team's expectations.

The final step before onboarding is an interview over lunch/coffee with me. This isn't always possible, so sometimes it is just a call, but nonetheless, I am the last person in line. This is a chance for me to see how they interact with other people in a social setting. By this point, they are far less guarded, and I get to see their real personality. How are their conversation skills? How are they treating the waiter/waitress? How do they behave when their order arrives late or perhaps incorrectly?

I ask questions like, "H*ow do you present and motivate patients to accept treatment plans?* Or, "H*ave you ever sold home care equipment to patients, like toothbrushes etc*.? I specifically use the word sold so I can gauge their reaction to having sales as part of their responsibilities. Lastly, I get a chance to ask them about their comfort level with certain tasks, their desired income target, goals and dreams. I want to find out if they have a vision for themselves or if they're just wandering aimlessly through their career.

Here is why this system works so well: I found out that one of the things I suck at is hiring people. I promise I will always be honest with you and a little vulnerable. I have over a 50% failure rate in choosing whom to hire in operations when it's exclusively left up to me.

I discovered I would hire people who were the most like me because I liked them (we were very similar) and not because they were right for the position. That is why failure rates climbed to about 50% or more. We have team members like our office managers who are much more effective at hiring and have a 70% success rate or higher. Who should be doing the hiring? We don't always follow this exactly, but the more we do, the more successful our hiring process becomes.

This process works extremely well when you already have a few key team members. If you are still a solopreneur or have a very small team and need to recruit for a position or two, it can be difficult to get a good outcome using internal resources. You will need to look for outside help. Perhaps you have a spouse who can assist. A spouse can be invaluable in this process because they know you well and have a keen insight into your weaknesses and shortfalls. Additionally, they have a vested interest in helping you find key employees who can help you build a high-performance practice. Not to mention an efficient business will make you happier when you come home to the family. You can also rely on your coaches and mentors to help you. Outside agencies can also be a resource.

***

My philosophy is always to hire for attitude and train for results. Here are the traits that I look for in people:

Integrity - This one is tough to find on the surface because you won't really know until you start to work with someone. Integrity, from my perspective, means a person does the right thing when no one is watching. It's that simple.

Hard Work – Typically, this is another buzzword that has lost a lot of meaning over the last 50 years. I define hard work by more than just the hours consumed. Hard work is my team members' desire to get out of their comfort zones and stay there long enough to improve. That work is hard. I am not looking to push someone so hard or spread them so thin they burn out or quit. I am talking about finding someone who is willing to put in the work to get the job done. Oftentimes I find they grew up on a farm, played competitive sports, volunteer their time for compassion projects, take pride in health and fitness, have children or enjoy a challenge. I don't have any data on this, but I have observed these things in our A-players. The more traits they exhibit, the better.

Intelligence - This is not a Grade-Point Average. Intelligence is not about how much a person knows, but their ability to learn and understand. An intelligent person can see similarities between two things that are apparently dissimilar. This is an amazing attribute. When you find this person, hire them and pay them well.

Intrinsic Motivation - People who know their own value find their motivation and satisfaction from completing challenging work for their own reasons.

Accountability - There are two types of accountability I seek. The first is owning their mistakes. This form of accountability, or lack thereof, becomes quickly apparent. A team member who feels confident enough to admit they have made a mistake and seek help to fix it and learn from it is easy to spot. They either do or they don't. The second type of accountability is what a person does when no one is looking. This form of accountability is very difficult to screen for, so we need to rely more on their other character traits.

Team Player - Every member of a high-functioning team has a role and contributes the best they can. The function of a team is well-documented, so there is little need to go into detail here. All I will add is that there is a compound effect when you put together a great team. A high-performing team doesn't necessarily require the most talented person in each role. It has more to do with how each team member can combine their efforts so that 1+1 = 3. Can this person function within our framework?

The burning question here is:

How do you figure out which people have these traits?

During the last stage of the application process mentioned above, I have a list of questions I ask that reveal these traits if they exist:

- What was the last challenge you inserted into your life?
- Why did you do that?
- What was your strategy?

For example, suppose a prospective recruit told me he decided to run a marathon because he wanted to push himself to do something difficult. Then he explained his training schedule and the changes to his nutritional regimen.

Do you think this individual has the capacity for hard work, an aptitude for learning and is intrinsically motivated? Yes, or yes? On the other hand, if that person is having difficulty answering and is skeptical about why anyone would add complexity or a challenge into their life, is likely not a good fit.

To gain more insight into teamwork and accountability you may ask:

- Describe a time you were working on a group project or a task with coworkers and it didn't work out.
- What happened?
- How did you manage/handle the outcome?
- What role did you play in arriving at that outcome?

Our system isn't perfect. I don't believe any recruitment system is. But ours has allowed us to create a dream team and minimize our turnover dramatically. Over the last five years we have seen less than 5% of our team seek employment elsewhere, including doctors. I believe this is multifactorial: an effective recruitment process, hiring for attitude not skill, effective leadership and an awesome culture.

It's a culture of fun, support, compassion and accountability, among other things. We all share a common vision and values. This is the key.

After all of this discussion about recruitment, I will leave you with this:

Of all the things we do, I think we are best at:

- Taking a genuine interest in our team.
- Treating them like equals.
- Trying to help them grow both inside and outside of work.

Our training and systems are not nearly as powerful as simply being compassionate and caring for everyone's well-being. We are a work family and I want to see each member of my team achieve happiness and fulfillment in their lives.

Ideas to Remember

- Teamwork makes the dream work.
- Focus on quality traits for each position.
- Deploy tools like the Kolbe Assessments.
- Involve the team in the hiring decisions.
- Hire for attitude and train for success.
- Invest in your team, be a great leader and create a fantastic culture.

CHAPTER NINE

Deeper Dive: Systems & Processes which will Help You Earn AND Retain More $$

"Let systems run the business
and people run the systems.
People come and go but the systems remain constant."
~Michael Gerber

Robert Kiyosaki, author of Rich Dad, Poor Dad, developed the cash flow quadrant. The concept explains that income can be generated as an Employee, Self-Employed, Business Owner or Investor. Income from the quadrants on the right are active while income from the left are residual.

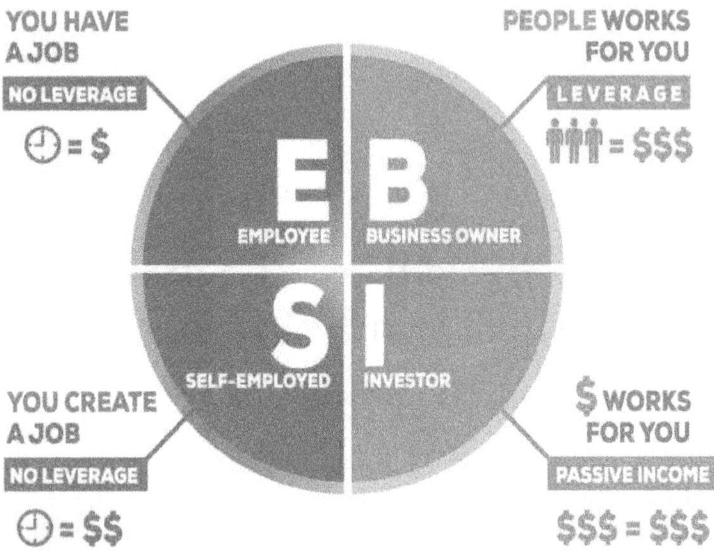

The single biggest difference between active versus residual income is leverage. Active income leverages your own time while residual sources leverages the time and resources of others. That is what Michael Gerber is saying here when he suggests that you let the system run your business and have your people run the system.

An effective system leverages the time and resources of others. In other words, you should not have to leverage your own time if you have a functioning system.

Systems & Processes which will Help You Earn AND Retain More $$$

The target is not how much money you make. It is how much money you keep. We have discussed cost control at length in Chapters Three and Seven I am going to shift gears a little bit here and give you a different perspective on how much your practice earns versus how much it keeps.

Khalid Saleh of *invesp* reports that it costs five times more to attract a new customer than it does to keep an existing one.[xii] That's a staggering figure! The other figure I find shocking is that 44% of companies have a greater focus on customer acquisition versus only 18% on retention. This makes absolutely no sense to me. However, assuming that the general survey results are statistically relevant for the dental industry, this presents a massive opportunity for you!

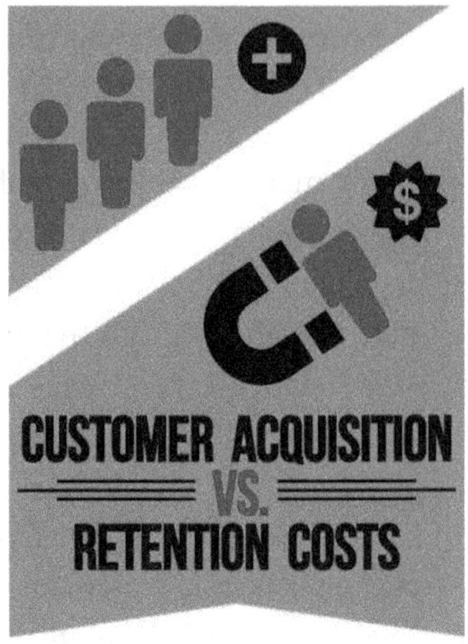
CUSTOMER ACQUISITION
VS.
RETENTION COSTS

It costs five times as much to attract a new customer, than to keep an existing one

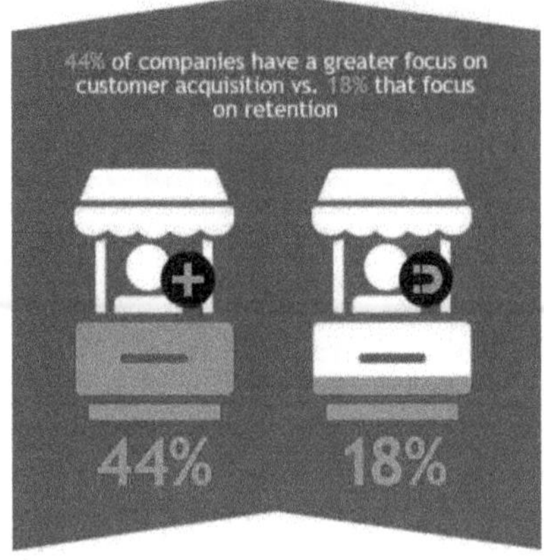
44% of companies have a greater focus on customer acquisition vs. 18% that focus on retention
44%
18%

Let's look at the numbers. These figures are strictly for illustration purposes and your actual figures may vary. Working off of the following assumptions:

- The Client Acquisition Cost is constant at $1000 per new client
- Average Lifetime Value of a new client is $7500 over 15 years
- The Client Retention Cost is 20%, or 1/5th that of the acquisition cost

Using the assumptions above, you would need to spend $1000 to attract a new client.

The Client Acquisition Cost (CAC) = Total # of new clients / Total sales and promotion expense

The Average Lifetime Value (LTV) is calculated at $2500 every five years and the average clients stays with a practice for approximately 15 years, which totals $7500.

LTV = Total Revenue / Total Clients

Assuming that this practice does not spend the $200 retention cost to keep a client, the client will only stay 10 years, leaving an opportunity cost of $2500. The total net value of a new client is $4000 (-1000 + $7500 - $2500).

Now assume that this practice invests the $200 retention cost to keep a client and the client will stay the full 15 years. That means this practice has spent $200 to earn another $2500 over the last five years of the client life with that practice.

Happy clients are more likely to refer someone when they know, like and trust the practice. Suppose the practice converts a referral from a happy client. The cost of the conversion is $0 while the lifetime value is $7500! Please keep in mind that this is an ultra-conservative figure and for demonstration purposes only.

	Attract New Clients	Retain Current Clients
Client Acquisition Cost	($1000)	
Client Retention Cost		($200)
Average Lifetime Value	$7500	
Opportunity Cost	($2500)	
Referral Value		$7500 ea.
Total Net Value	$4000	$7300

To compare the two strategies, the ROI on attracting new clients is 4x ($4000/$1000) while the ROI on retention is 12.5x ($15000/$1200). The retention return is so much higher because the practice earns:

- The full $7500 on the original client
- $7500 on the referral
- Less the original $1000 acquisition
- Less the $200 retention expense

Now that you have read through Chapter Four and you know your numbers, what would the ROI comparison look like for your practice? It's exciting to think about.

What is even more exciting to think about is how a high-performing practice implements strategies to retain more clients and earn more income.

Let me show you.

Client Retention

The WKY

You might have heard of a KYC or Know Your Client form that is used in financial services. If you have invested money anywhere at any time, you have most likely signed one. The KYC is a document requirement that includes vital contact information about you, as well as some of your investing habits. The purpose is to demonstrate a fiduciary duty and get to know about the clients.

In practice, the KYC is for CYA or Covering Your Ass. The document is rarely used for anything that furthers the relationship with a client.

That's why we adopted the WKY or *We Know You* intake form. We collect some vital contact information about our clients, as well as medical history. The WKY actually has an additional function and helps us develop a relationship with new clients and to strengthen relationship with current clients. We can do that because the WKY also collects information about what inspires our clients, lists some of their favorite hobbies, authors or restaurants.

The reality is some people give the form a puzzled look and ask if they need to fill out all the information. We explain relationships are important to us and we feel like when we understand our clients beyond demographics and histories, we can connect on a different level to provide them with the best possible treatment.

Who would say no to an offer like that? Using the WKY as a tool in this manner enables us to deliver a WOW experience for our patients. This allows us to quickly reconnect with them at subsequent visits and choose topics they enjoy. We can present them with a book from their favorite author at the cessation of treatment. Once they receive their final restorations for implants or cosmetic treatment, we can gift them a dinner at their favorite restaurant. This is a level of attention that would serve well for High-Value Patients (HVP) such as orthodontics, implants and cosmetics, to name a few.

That's the level of thinking we work on. We genuinely want to know our patients. A high-performance practice does more than just fix up the patients' teeth and send them out the door. That is what customer retention is all about. This doesn't mean you have to buy each of your patients dinner or a book, although we recommend that for High-Value Treatments (HVT). We are simply emphasizing the importance of taking a genuine interest in your patients. Simply remembering small details about them goes a long way, even in the absence of a gift. People like to feel connected and appreciated instead of being looked upon merely as a line item.

Minimizing Team Turnover

As far as your patients are concerned, the quality of your office is determined by employee retention. As mentioned in the previous chapter, selecting the right team, taking a genuine interest in them, investing in their training and empowering them to use their best judgment goes a long way in reducing staff turnover. Retaining patients is directly correlated with minimizing staff turnover because the message we're delivering to patients is *consistency.* How would the patient experience change if there was a different receptionist or treatment coordinator every time they came to the office? If there's a revolving door of staff, the patient may experience an unstable environment and start to question why they should be there if they are seeing a new face all the time. Happy staff creates a fun and positive work environment; The ultimate payoff is a great patient experience and ultimately retention.

Here are some Examples of Customer Service Protocols:

- WKY: Listed above in detail.
- Greet clients by their first name and with a smile (take photos for patient chart)
- Offer them coffee or tea.
- Doctor greets them in the waiting room with a handshake.

- Provide an office tour.
- Introduce a new-patient gift delivered at the cessation of the exam.
- Offer a warm towel, neck pillow or blanket during treatment.
- Ensure their favorite TV show, Netflix or music station is playing during treatment.
- Send them a birthday card every year, signed personally by each team member with a gift card/voucher for free dessert.
- Complete comfort checks throughout treatment appointments. Always asking how patients are doing. ~Use a signal to start--thumbs up or down for example. That way they are not wondering how they are supposed to communicate comfort or discomfort to you.
- Stay on time! If you happen to run behind, address it immediately by going out to the waiting room to explain. Then move the client into an operatory and put on a TV show or music of their liking and have an assistant get started on some level of their treatment. Do not be disrespectful of people's time, or you are indirectly saying *my time is more important than yours*, which is never good. If someone arrives early to the office for an appointment, do everything you can to get them back right away.
- Never have anyone interrupt a patient mid-treatment. For example, your assistant enters the operatory to explain they are ready for you in

Room Two. Nothing says *you're just a number* more than this.

- Do not rush into your appointments. Instead, learn to be efficient with the dentistry. Give people the time they desire and deserve before and after treatment is initiated and completed.
- Do not forget about them after the transaction: Complete post op calls for all patients that have received local anesthetic. We recommend the doctor do these personally.

The entire purpose of this level of engagement is simply connecting with people and delivering more value to them than anybody else. That's it. Remember, we can't control whether or not clients choose our practice. We only control our activity, which can influence their decision to stay once they have chosen us. If we have done our job, we have built a ton of value, we will probably have our clients for life. That is because of how we make our clients feel. People do not remember what you say to them, but they do remember how you made them feel. Great customer service makes people feel valued and important.

Painless and Profound Anesthesia, Efficiency and Durability

The title is self-explanatory. Give painless local anesthetic that lasts the course of treatment. NO pain. With a little practice anyone can do this. We can be caring and as gentle as possible, but if there is still pain there, clients will avoid you at all costs. One thing all human beings have in common is the avoidance of pain. That's why it is so important to take every extra step to make our patients feel as little pain as possible. If the last memory of a patient is pain and suffering, client retention is going to suffer. At that point, you're just another dentist.

Fast and good are not mutually exclusive. Think of a pit team in NASCAR. They have practiced their routine so they can deliver a high-quality result in a fraction of the time. Training, practice and well-defined roles and responsibilities will help you deliver high-quality dentistry in a fraction of the time. The quicker the treatment, the less trauma and therefore less post-op discomfort, which minimizes the potential for pain and discomfort. Durability and longevity are the last pieces.

Do good work. Period!

****IMPORTANT****

Painless, efficient and durable dentistry is a must. If your work hurts or fails or treatment times are excessive, customer service alone will not keep them coming back.

I have learned many of these concepts from amazing and outrageously successful people like Anthony Robbins, Jim Rohn and Robin Sharma. I surround myself with these thought leaders by reading their books, listening to their podcasts and attending their events.

I get the benefit of thousands of years of teaching and experience through the content I consume. One of the most valuable lessons each of these leaders have taught me is that the simplest form of the idea is usually the best option. Dentists--and people in general--tend to overcomplicate things, when all we really need to do is spend more time on the relationship and more time on the value generation for each patient. Believe it or not, an investment in improved communication techniques, relationship management and customer service will help your practice grow more than a Cone Beam CT, Cerec, or additional clinical C.E. Most of the time, the problem is not the lack of technology or the fact that you are not educated enough or have enough letters behind your name. It's your inability to understand what people really want, the ability to influence them to accept treatment so you can enrich their lives.

Make their experience memorable and make them feel good and your chances of client retention will go through the roof.

That is when high-performing practices make a shift. They no longer have the same problems as the average dental office. While other dental offices are struggling and focusing exclusively on trying to attract more new patients while their current clientele are leaving out the back door frustrated and dissatisfied, the high-performing practice invests in its relationships with their patients. Their client retention is high and conversion on their treatment plans rise with the level of trust from their patients.

Phasing Treatment to Build Trust

Most of us get hung up on the ortho, the cosmetics or other comprehensive treatment plans. This is great. The more you know, the more you see, and it's your responsibility to teach patients about the treatment options available to them (SEE PCSS TECHNIQUE). However, it is also important not to be pushy in a stereotypical used-car salesman way. It's better to be supportive. It is okay to do the filling instead of the crown or one crown at a time, and so on.

The good news is if you deliver a solution for their biggest chief complaint, it's okay to do a $100, $200, $300 or $400 treatment, because at some point, they're going to come back to you for $5000 worth of braces or multiple crowns. If they tell you the color of their front teeth bothers them, give them the whitening and then let them know they can come back for their next cleaning. There is no need to get hung up on the entire treatment plan because the lifetime value is so much more important. Give them what they want--phase treatment. I will caution this--phasing treatment does not mean supervised neglect. It doesn't mean we shy away from telling patients what the problems are, the consequences of going without treatment and the solutions available. It just means we address the priority areas first and don't present everything at once, which may be overwhelming.

A supportive dialogue we use in our office all the time is as follows:

> *"We understand this is a lot of information coming at you. Please don't let it overwhelm you. We are here to answer any questions you have. You can also do as little or as much of this as you like at one time. We often deal with areas that are likely to cause pain and infection first. Then we begin thinking about cosmetics or structure/function problems like crooked or missing teeth. We will support whatever decision you make"*

For patients presenting with multiple issues and those who are totally insurance-driven, this statement will help retain them over the long haul versus having them running for the hills, only to find themselves in the arms of another dentists who says,

> *"They recommended what? Oh, that's way too much. You just need a couple of fillings and that's all."*

We all know who we are talking about. Let's not be one of those.

If you are genuine and honest about the relationship and give before you get, you will be handsomely rewarded. The currency of the relationship game is referrals. The cost of acquisition is zero and the lifetime value of a client referral is massive. As you read earlier in this chapter, the return on a referral client is more than three times the return of a new client. The only investments required from you is time and value. If not for more money, do it for more fulfillment. Treating people like gold makes you feel like gold. The appreciation, significance and validation that comes from this overshadows money for me all day long. The interesting thing is the more I chase fulfillment through enriching the lives of others, the more money I make. Who would have thunk it?

New Patient Acquisition and Reactivation

For obvious reasons, most of this chapter has been focused on client retention--the investment is much lower to keep a client and the return is much higher. High-performance practices balance both sides of patient flow. This business really is simple.

- Get people in the door.
- Get them to buy from you.
- Get them to come back.
- Make more than you spend.

That's it. No business in the world, including dentistry, is any more complicated than that. Simplicity isn't necessarily easy. This last piece is a focus on business development or getting people in the door.

Before we jump neck deep into strategies and tactics, a quick review of the brand continuum from Chapter Four:

Brand Absence | Brand Awareness | Brand Preference | Brand Insistence | Brand Advocacy

Client retention strategies move patients from *brand preference* through to *brand advocacy.* In short, create a patient base who feels so valued and so appreciated by you that they chose to rave about it to others.

Reactivation strategies focus on the client who may have dipped back into *brand absence* but are most likely hovering in *brand awareness*. The target of these strategies is to move clients up into *brand preference*.

New patient acquisition strategies thrive almost exclusively in *brand absence* and the target is to move a client into *brand awareness*.

The task for you and your marketing team is to match the strategy to where in your client journey your target prospect resides.

New Patient Acquisition

At the start of the client journey with your high-performance practice, the prospective patient is found in *brand absence*. In other words, they don't know who you are or what your value proposition is. Overcoming the challenge of awareness requires frequency and timing. The frequency you can control, but the timing requires a little bit of luck.

If I introduced you to some of my marketing friends, they would tell you that you are going to need five-to-seven touchpoints before a person will take any action. A touch point is any interaction of value with your practice. Touchpoints include emails, phone calls/messages, impressions (views of an advertisement or other piece of content), website, mail and meetings, to name a few. The rule of thumb is it will take any five-to-seven touchpoints to get to an action, even if it results in a *no thank-you.* You could email someone seven times or call them seven times. The effect of too many of one thing can be annoying, so the ideal tactic would mix two or three mediums to connect five-to-seven times.

Here is a list of external marketing tools and tactics you can use to increase the number of touchpoints with your group of prospective clients:

Local Celebrity	**Get Published**	**Speaking Engagements**
- Branding by association with celebrities - Media Relations - Sponsorship	- White papers - Blog posts - Articles	- Local Chamber of Commerce - Trade Shows - Corporate Events
Publicity	**Media**	**Advertising & Promotions**
- Charity work (board membership) - Scholarships - Community programs - Youth programs	- YouTube - Facebook - Instagram - Pinterest - Twitter - PR - Podcasting	- Print (Newspaper, Magazines) - Digital (Display, Search) - SEO/SEM - Direct Mail - Influencers (Google Reviews) - Affiliates - Joint Ventures

This is not an exhaustive list by any means. Whichever combination of tools, tactics or platforms you choose, you need to know your numbers. The success of any outreach relies on a plan that defines who you want to reach, what you want them to do (call to action), what is your baseline for measurement (cost per thousand impressions, opt-in rate, engagement rate, closing rate, cost of acquisition, lead source ROI) and campaign timeline.

Each of these measures will yield a result you can compare to each other. Some modalities will take longer than others to yield results. Some modalities need to be split-tested by having multiple versions delivered to different prospects to compare response. As we discussed earlier, the only way to eat an elephant is one bit at a time. No need to launch all of your campaigns at once, especially if you have little-to-no experience in marketing.

Whether you have an internal team, or you hire an outside team to help you, here are some important questions you need to ask:

- What's the predicted total spend for the duration of the campaign? Is it capped?
- What are the predicted milestone measurements (impressions, click-throughs, opt-ins)
- How are these measures going to be tracked?
- What is the expected ROI on the total ad spend in dollars? In new clients?

The three prerequisites you need to have when launching any campaign are *time*, *patience* and *money*. Make sure you have plenty of each.

Most dentists do not understand marketing. I certainly did not until I had an opportunity to learn from the best and brightest minds--Abraham, Kennedy, Robbins, Brunson, Kern and many others. I have taken this information, simplified it and turned it into material that is applicable for dental offices. Our offices have grown tremendously as a result of marketing intelligently, in spite of being located in saturated markets. It's not your job to get a PhD in marketing. For me, it's become an obsession. You might just want to get more new patients through the door. The bottom line is that an educated client is a better client. Therefore, learning a thing or two about marketing will help you not only become a better consumer, but a better client for your vendors. This is a win-win.

Quick Tip

Plan your marketing budget and modalities for the entire year and create a marketing calendar from this information.

Patient Reactivation

An inactive patient is one who has not visited your practice within the last 18 months.

There can be many reasons why a patient goes inactive—they've moved, are deceased, have forgotten to rebook, or they didn't value the service and went elsewhere. Whatever the reason may be, you don't know what you don't know.

These patients were your clients at one point. They are not necessarily in the *brand absence* part of the client journey. They are most likely in the brand awareness category. A successful outreach campaign for clients in this category will need the luck of timing. They have already had an experience with your practice and hopefully it wasn't a poor experience. The timing of your materials is important because you must first reintroduce your practice. Then the patient must feel they need some dental work within a short time of receiving your materials.

THIS IS NOT A ONE-AND-DONE STRATEGY

This is an outline of the reactivation process:

- Print and manage your 18-month attrition list daily. There are software solutions that can do this for you.
- Reach out to the patients via phone using a script.

Sample Script:

"Hi John, this is Debby from XYZ Dental. How are you doing?" Wait for answer (WFA).

"It's been while since we have seen you for a dental cleaning in our office. Dr J asked me to give you a call and get you in for an appointment. Dr. J has extended a special offer to you for a free get 'reacquainted' exam. We have Thursday at (Time) and next Tuesday at (Time). Which of those works best for you?"

If neither of those times work, offer two additional times. Do not ask them when they would like to come in. It is important you give them just two options at a time. If they are busy or do not have a calendar or they're driving, simply ask them what's the best time to call them back and ensure you do so.

If they accept one of the times given, also ask them if they would like to book their cleaning with the hygienist since they are coming in to meet Dr. J anyway.

This is one example of a few scripts we use to maximize conversion during reactivation.

If you are unable to get a live patient on the phone or have left a voicemail with no reply, send out a letter with information related to importance of S/RP, Perio or Oral Systemic Health on an envelope marked *High Priority* or

Confidential. This information would be accompanied by a letter signed by the dentist.

Follow up two weeks after the letter was sent via phone to determine if it was received and whether the patient has any questions. In this circumstance, you can leave a voicemail and request a call back.

Sample Script:

"Hi John, this is Debby from XYZ Dental. I sent out an important package to you a few weeks back and I wanted to ensure you received it. Please give me a call at your earliest convenience and ask for me directly. Again, this is Debby from XYZ Dental. I look forward to receiving your call and have a great day!"

At this stage, we leave the ball in the patient's court. It is my belief that a patient who does not make the next move is either avoiding us, had a bad experience, moved or is now seeking care at another office. If you do not hear from them within two weeks, simply inactivate/archive the patient.

Quick Tip

Minimize the need for reactivation by implementing of the following:

~ Intelligent reappointment process. 85-95% of hygiene patients should leave with their next appointment scheduled.
~ Immediately seek a reappointment for SNC and No-Shows.
~I have yet to see an office at 100%, so there will always be patients to reactivate. However, getting into the habit of booking the next appointment before the patient leaves is best practice. Train your hygiene team and track their individual results.

High-performance practices will go deep before they go wide. In other words, they will get really proficient at two-to-three tactics before they add any other modalities. Wherever you are in your practice today, the only mistake you can make at this point is not to try.

Ideas to Remember

- The cash flow quadrant from which you derive income determines if the income is active or residual.
- The biggest difference between active income (job, self-employed) and residual income (business owner, investor) is leverage.
- New client acquisition is five times more expensive than client retention.
- The *We Know You* form is used to increase the level of client services.
- Minimizing staff turnover, effective customer service protocols and phasing treatments are all key components for retaining more patients/clients.
- The lifetime value of a referral client is more than three times the return of a new client.
- New patient acquisition requires *brand absence*-level marketing programs.
- The goal of your system is to move a patient/client from *brand absence* through to *brand advocacy.*
- Patient reactivation can be another source of incremental income with minimal expense.

CHAPTER TEN

Be the Dumbest Person in the Room

"There is no better game in the world
when you are in good company,
and no worse game when you are in bad company."
~Tommy Bolt

This quote from Tommy Bolt is the perfect way to kick off this chapter about being the dumbest guy in the room. If you're not familiar with Tommy Bolt's story, he was an accomplished PGA Tour golfer who won 15 titles, including one major at the 1958 U.S. Open. He didn't join the tour until his 30's, well after serving in the United States Army in WWII. The most interesting part of his story is not his achievement as a professional golfer. He was better known for his temper around the links. His nicknames include *The Thunder* and *Terrible Tommy*. He had a reputation for tantrums, breaking his clubs and throwing them into water hazards.

This quote suggests how golf can be the worst game when you're in bad company is fitting because Terrible Tommy was often the bad company. Tommy's story fits well into the topic of this closing chapter about who you put yourself into close company with.

Imagine if you were on the course with Tommy during his prime and had to contend with his rants. I am sure his attitude and energy would affect your game. I think I can safely assume that any other tour players paired up with Tommy probably didn't have their best rounds on those days.

Another way to position this chapter is if you are the smartest person in the room, you're in the wrong room. The point being, who are you surrounding yourself with? Are the people in that room leveling up your game, or are they dragging you down like a Thunderbolt? I am not suggesting you only subject yourself to these environments. There is something to be said about surrounding yourself by three different categories of people:

- Those farther behind the times as you. Help them achieve their goals.
- Those who are in the same place as you. Mastermind with them.
- Those who are farther ahead on the timeline. Shut up and listen. When you are the dumbest person in the room, you will learn a ton, collapse timelines and get ten times your results.

If you are thinking:

Hey wait a minute. Is he saying you can only learn from those at the same stage or ahead on the timeline as you?

Not at all. I have learned from people at all stages, but there's only one of these three groups from whom you will learn the most and maximize your results by ten times. The third group.

Before you start to think I am being rude, I don't believe anyone is dumb. I do believe there are the learned and unlearned. The unlearned tend to do a lot of talking and very little listening. As I said earlier in the book, success leaves clues (Jim Rohn), so get in rooms with people who have accomplished what you are looking to accomplish, listen, ask good questions and then execute. Being the dumbest person in the room will help you make more money in less time.

If You Think You Know It All, You have Failed.

I learned this lesson hard and fast. I had just graduated from dental school and had achieved something that less than 3% of the population has done. Just like you, I was grinding away to get my degree, and of course come out on the other side Dr. B. This was one of the biggest accomplishments in my life to that point and I was proud. So now I had the education, a title and a ton of ambition. I had a lot of confidence but struggled with ego. I always wanted to be the smartest guy around and share all the information I'd learned with anyone who would listen. I was talking more than listening.

Even when I was in a conversation, I was that guy who they talk about in communications training. You know the one--that guy who is just thinking about the next thing he wants to say instead of listening to the other person.

Then something clicked for me and I figured out that those who listen the most, learn the most. Just because I already know something, so what? Telling people what I know wasn't helping me learn any more. The only way I could continue learning was to add to what I already knew instead of constantly talking about what I thought I knew. I had to break that habit loop of always talking too much about what I knew. For me at the time, I felt it was the only way to prove my worth. All that just got in the way of me learning. My natural inclination is to help. I feel like if I know something I should share it immediately in hopes it will be of tremendous value to others. This is the exact reason I am writing this book. What I am suggesting is not withholding information, but just checking in and ensuring you are listening and learning at all times. The best communicators are those who learn to listen.

When you think you know everything, you're not listening to people. That also means you're not listening to the bad things that are going on around you. You straight-up miss all the subtle cues that let you know trouble is about to happen or that a major problem is brewing. You stand to gain a tremendous benefit by having an open mind and always being ready to listen, learn and absorb information

I've made every mistake in the book because I thought I knew how to do everything. I can think of a hundred mistakes I made when I first came out of dental school, opened my first office, negotiated deals, bought supplies and equipment, looked for the right real estate and found the right partners. I caused myself a lot of stress and financial loss as a result of what I thought I knew.

You Don't Know What You Don't Know

Herein lies the failure when you think you know it all. You really don't know if you don't know something. There are lots of things we know we don't know. For example, I know I have no clue how to hard-code a software program. I know I do not know how build a scaffold safely. I can probably go and learn something about those fields if I was interested enough. But I already know the things I have no clue how to do.

Where transformational growth lives is in those AHA moments, when we learn about something we had no idea even existed. Call it a revelation, epiphany, discovery or whatever. I experience these moments a couple of times a day because I am listening for them. I don't know what they are or when they will show up, but I know they are out there.

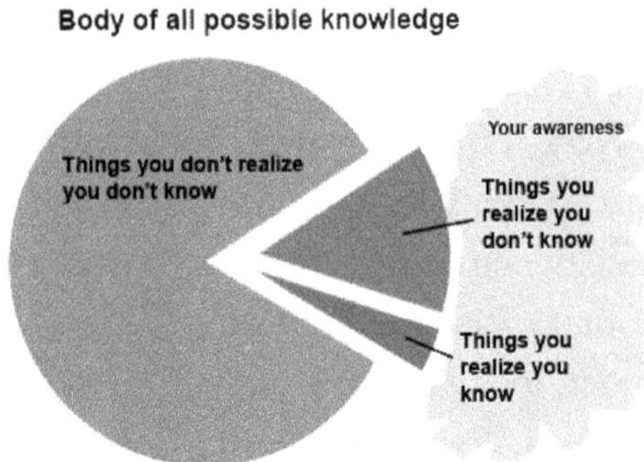

As dentists, we generally know how to diagnose the basics when we come into dental school. Then we take a few courses or continuing education courses and now we're empowered with knowledge. Putting that to use is powerful because we have so much more clarity in our next clinical exam. Suddenly, we can see problems we didn't see before because we weren't conditioned to see it before. You take an implant program and suddenly all you see is missing teeth! You take an ortho program and all you see is malocclusion!

This is just a clinical example and seems obvious. After all, that's why we go to dental school, is to learn from people who have done it successfully in the past. Exactly! This is how you need to treat your business if you want to have a high-performance practice. You will need to abandon any notion that you know it all and adopt a mindset that even though you know a lot, you have even more to learn.

***

Remember I said you will learn more from people farther ahead in the timeline than you? That is true. The problem is, you don't always know who is in that position. That's why prejudging people is a fatal mistake. The worst kind of mistake you can make is when you don't know that you have made one. At least when you have a serious lapse in judgment and there is some sort of consequence, like embarrassment or some sort of loss, you know you did something wrong.

I made a major mistake by prejudging, but thankfully I figured it out and was able to correct it. I was at a conference and walked into the room all cocky because I have read some Tony Robbins books and built a couple of businesses. I was eager to share all my knowledge and have people listen to me. I walked into the event and noticed an older guy around 70 years old chatting with a few people and looking like a lonely old man talking someone's ear off.

We made eye-contact. All I could think was, "Great. Now it's my turn." This gentleman wanted to chat, and he was giving some free and unsolicited advice. I was doing my usual routine of thinking about what I was going to say next or try to get out of the conversation. I didn't invest any attention or value on him. Then about five minutes later another attendee came up to me and asked what Jerry and I were talking about. I was so disinterested I had to ask who Jerry was. That's when my colleague explained that Jerry was worth about $2.5 billion. All I could think was how oblivious I'd been.

I made a lot of those mistakes in the past and have learned from them. My wife has taught me a lot about this. She would ask me, "Why do you write people off like that?" My response was, "I am not writing them off. I just value my time." This is also one of my biggest regrets. I am a loving and kind person. I enjoy people. Why did I write people off? It's because I was so focused on what I know. I was a know-it-all, not a learn-it-all. You never know who you're sitting beside.

Millionaires and billionaires don't walk around with a sign around their necks with their net worth posted on it. In fact, they rarely dress the part at all. It's usually the guy who is super decked out that is broke. Hang around the guy who is wearing the t-shirt and jeans and you might be sitting next to the next Mark Cuban or Zuckerberg.

You are going to learn so much from other people that it just makes sense for you to get to know as many people as possible. You cannot simply take, take, take. The most effective way is to attend conferences or join a mastermind where you know there are likeminded people.

You'll never miss an uncovered opportunity when you accept people without judgment.

By the way, I did go back and connect with Jerry and we had a nice lunch together. He was an amazing wealth of knowledge and extremely humble. I have had an opportunity to meet multiple millionaires and a few billionaires. None of them are in it for the money--just what the money can do.

***

I SURROUND MYSELF WITH PEOPLE SMARTER THAN ME

I surround myself with people I look up to and admire. It allows me to further grow and learn from them plus we always have something interesting to talk about. I love their entrepreneurial drive and love hearing about their new endeavours.

I had the opportunity to meet all of my mentors and we became good friends.

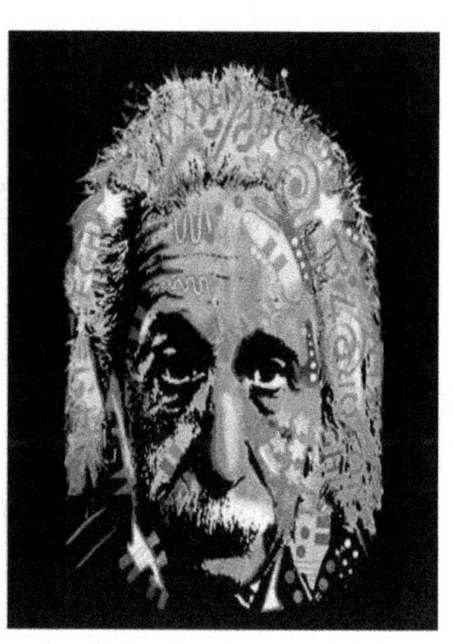

If it's good enough for Einstein, it's good enough for pretty much everybody. We touched on the subject in Chapter Eight and I would like to dive a little deeper in the subject of surrounding yourself with people who are more learned than you.

If you're the most learned person in your circle, you're learning nothing. What you have in your head right now has already served you. You will not be able to achieve any more with what you know at the moment. You will need to change something in the way you think in order to change who you are and what you can achieve. That may require learning something completely new, or just getting a different perspective about something you already know. Everyone has something they can teach us, and we can learn something from everyone.

When I'm in a room full of people who are experts in an area or who have done something even 1% better than I have or 5% better than I have, I go into learning mode. That marginal difference between our respective achievements can make a significant impact on my results. They share their successes and I apply what I learned. Within a month, I will have grown by 1 to 5% as a result of their sharing.

All you have to do is get into the right room. Most dentists are struggling to bring in new patients. They agonize over the marketing plan they need to get in place and build it up to be a bigger and more complicated task then it needs to be. That's the moment they need to get into a room full of people who know more about marketing than they do. They will likely meet someone who has had the same problem and perhaps they'll share what they did to attract 15 new patients a month for six months by doing just one thing in only 20 minutes per day.

Where are you more likely to have conversations like that? In a room full of people at your level or less or in room of people more learned than you?

Now that you've found a room of people who have learned more than you, make sure it is the right room. If you want to attract more patients, be in a room full of expert marketers. Want to become a better dentist? Find a room with highly skilled doctors. Hanging out in a room full of physics PhD's might not serve you as well, even though they know more about their subject of expertise.

Once you find that room and shift into learning mode, double down. Go all-in to glean as much as you can handle and functionally implement.

The Wheel has already been Invented

When you've found a room of people smarter than you and it's the right room, don't reinvent the wheel. Success leaves clues and all you need to do is follow the trail.

Observe the people who are successful and deconstruct what they've done. Follow those habits. If you're being totally honest with yourself and are doing the work, you will be able to grow a high-performance practice. It's not a secret. The person you are modeling likely did the same with other successful people they respect and admire. The problem is that we think our way is better and we want to reinvent the wheel. Here is another honest moment between us. If your way was better, you would already have the practice and lifestyle you wanted.

The More You Learn, The More You Earn

If you have someone in front of you who has done something that is worth modeling and you want it, stop talking. It doesn't matter what you know. You are already going to leave with that information. You don't need to prove to this person how much you know. All you need to do is take pearls of wisdom from this individual and go and apply it. Use it as a learning opportunity instead of an opportunity to sell yourself. Shut up and listen. Stop selling yourself. At this moment, nobody needs to hear what is in your mind, because you're there to learn.

You may be thinking that you do listen. The next question to ask yourself is do you apply what you've heard? Do you resist it? The next time you are listening, try and pay attention to the times you stop listening or were angry or frustrated with what the individual was saying. I have learned the most about myself when I understand these moments. They were often when the presenter was stating facts I already knew but I either failed in the area or didn't apply that knowledge in the past. That's when the guilt, anxiety and subsequent anger or disengagement sets in. Pay attention to that voice in your head and your emotions. It can be a tremendous benefit to help you get out of your own way and open up the floodgates to your future success and prosperity.

Warren Buffet reads five hours a day. Billionaire Bill Gates reads a book a week and has said that if he could have one superpower, it would to be able to read faster. Anthony Robbins has read thousands of books. The examples go on and on.

Growing a high-performance practice and becoming part of the top 5% doesn't happen by default. It is manufactured by design. The goal is to learn from those who have preceded us so we can grow. *The more you learn, the more you earn* is pretty simple concept. Now, there is one caveat to that, which is the more you learn and apply, the more you earn. Knowledge is not power unless you use it.

Always be a Student

To be studious is a state of being. There is something next level about being a student. The most successful people on the planet operate with a beginner's mindset. Always be learning and you will never miss an opportunity to grow personally or professionally.

That being said, we must apply what we have learned in order to make change. As dentists, more information and knowledge can be addictive. The key to progress and growth is to continue learning and executing simultaneously. Learn, apply, measure results, course correct if necessary, and repeat. You will learn equally if not more in the execution than in the gathering of information.

I know I've already mentioned this, but I believe it is important enough to mention again. Something a lot of dentists have in common is they hear or read something like always be a student and they think….

"I am and always have been. I do a billion hours of Continuing Education each year, I am diplomat of XYZ, I have a cone beam, laser and cerec capabilities in my office. I have learned, learned, learned. My office is still only breaking even or it's losing money, I don't have enough patients or my staff sucks. It's everything else, and it has nothing to do with the fact I haven't learned enough".

I agree with them. It is frustrating to have all this knowledge you want to apply and not be able to do so because of a lack of knowledge in other areas. That's right. They are unable to do so because they have been focused on the wrong things, like more dental CE and more technology instead of leadership, culture, communication, marketing and management training.

They have been in the wrong rooms and have surrounded themselves with the wrong people. There is nothing wrong with more dental CE or more technology and I endorse both. However, I am just saying you must learn at least as much of the other stuff, the stuff that will grow your business ten times and allow you to actually pay back the vendors for your fancy equipment or pay down your student loan or CE tuition. If you don't want to learn about the other stuff, be an associate for someone else who has, form a strategic partnership with someone who does or come to terms with the fact that your office will be a constant stress in your life.

I have been fortunate to mastermind with numerous millionaires and elite performers in both business and dentistry. Each has had a major impact and contribution leading to where I am now. Had I not paid to learn from them, I would not own a fraction of what I now have.

There is a massive amount of information available from people that you can get for free. I happen to pay for much of it because I want to sit down and talk to people and have conversations. One of the best ways to get all the pearls from anyone is to invest in their products or services. I did that because I wanted front-row seats to them. As I mentioned before, I have also had the opportunity to meet a few billionaires and speak with them at length. My goals don't include becoming a billionaire, but I am so grateful I got to ask really good questions. I've also had a short discussion with Jeff Hoffman from Priceline.com. The amount of information I picked up in those few minutes was amazing. I learned three things from Jeff--talk to everybody, don't judge anyone and always be curious.

I also learned my number one job as an entrepreneur is to become a problem-solver. The bigger the problem you solve, the more people you help and the more money you make. At the end of the day, it's not about the money as much as it's about the impact you've had and what the money can do for your family, your team, and your community.

Your Career is a Journey

You're going to win. You're going to lose. People are going to resist you. People are going to make fun of you. People are going to disagree with you, argue and challenge you. People are going to love you. You're going to impact people both positively and negatively, but hopefully more positively. You're going to enrich people's lives. You're going to accomplish much more than just making money. So just enjoy the process.

It's important to have goals. It's important to seek the outcome you want. But if you're only obsessed with the outcome, you will forget about what's most important--building relationships.

Your career is not a destination where you reach the end with a sigh of relief that you've made it. It's the journey along your chosen path. At some point, you will look back and observe how far you've come. Take moments to pause and observe the impact you're having. Celebrate your wins along the way.

This journey is the long game so enjoy the process while you're playing. None of us can predict what's in store for us. Mitt Romney said, "Life has way too much chance and serendipity to be assured fame or fortune." If you enjoy the process, you will never have lost, right? It's going be hard work. Some days you're going to sweat and you're going to want to tear your hair out, but guess what? That's all part of it, because your pain and your struggle is your gift. The way I see it is, if I don't progress and achieve my goals I will suffer with the pain of regret. I chose to suffer through the pain of progress and success. Les Brown says, "If we are going to feel pain anyway, you might as well get some yardage out of it!"

Ideas to Remember

- Be the dumbest person in the room. If you are the smartest person in the room, you're in the wrong room.
- 80% of possible knowledge are things you don't realize you don't know.
- You never know who you are sitting beside.
- Don't recreate the wheel.
- Knowledge is not power, applied knowledge is power.
- Always be a student.
- The journey is a long game.

ONE LAST MESSAGE

Congratulations!

It is not common for dentists and practice owners to invest in their learning and development. Surprised? In fact, approximately only 30% do more than meet the minimum requirements set out by their governing body. It is even more uncommon for dentists to focus on business development as opposed to just clinical C.E. I truly admire and respect you for wanting to increase your knowledge and improve your business, leadership and life by reading the strategies, examples, and personal stories in this book.

My mission with this book was to serve you and make a positive difference in your life by presenting information that stimulates you to think and act differently.

My hope is that you have learned something new that you can apply today to get you one step closer to where you want to be. Whether you reach your goals is entirely up to you. No one can promise or guarantee what level of success you will achieve. However, by continuing to invest in yourself and by following some simple habits and strategies like those in this book, you can begin to craft the career, practice, or life you desire.

YOU CAN DO IT!

BEGIN TODAY WITHOUT DELAY ☺

I will leave you with a few quotes I hope inspire you!

"The investment which yields the highest returns is an investment in yourself."
~Warren Buffet

"Education is what remains after one has forgotten what one has learned in school."
~Albert Einstein

"All growth starts at the end of your comfort zone."
~Tony Robbins

"Success in business and life comes from consistent execution and the ability to stay focused despite the failures, obstacles and distractions which may come your way."
~Dr. Justin Bhullar

HPP
HIGH
PERFORMANCE
PRACTICE

Lead Generation Strategies					
1	Direct Mail	20	Affinity marketing	39	Paid Search
2	Print Advertising	21	Agents	40	Podcasting
3	Social Media Advertising	22	Blogs	41	Postcards
4	Referral Systems	23	Bookalogs	42	Premiums and Gifts
5	Joint Ventures	24	Catalogues	43	Product Placement
6	Word of Mouth	25	Consignment Selling	44	Promotions
7	Telemarketing	26	Contests and Sweepstakes	45	Reactivate Old Leads
8	Qualified Lists	27	Corporate Hospitality	46	Resellers
9	Networking	28	Database Marketing	47	Salespeople
10	Circle of Leverage	29	Demonstrations	48	Sampling
11	Paid Search	30	Dream 100 Clients	49	Search Engine Optimization
12	Become a Recognized Authority	31	eBay	50	Seminars
13	Public Relations	32	Experiental Marketing	51	Set Buying Criteria
14	Publicity	33	Franchising	52	Social Media Visibility
15	Brochures	34	Line Extensions	53	Sponsorship
16	Newsletters	35	Link Building	54	Testimonials
17	Leaflet Drops or Inserts	36	Magalogs	55	Viral Marketing
18	Exhibitions & Trade Shows	37	Mini Media	56	Websites
19	Card Deck Offers	38	Offers	57	Search Engine Marketing

---

[i] Davidson, E. (2017, July 24). The Average Time to Reach Profitability in a Start Up Company. Retrieved May 10, 2018, from http://smallbusiness.chron.com/average-time-reach-profitability-start-up-company-2318.htm

[ii] https://www.investopedia.com/slide-show/top-6-reasons-new-businesses-fail/

[iii] http://www.dentistryiq.com/articles/2015/07/communicating-trust-the-key-to-dental-case-acceptance.html

[iv] UCL News (Ed.). (2009, August 04). How long does it take to form a habit? Retrieved July 8, 2018, from http://www.ucl.ac.uk/news/news-articles/0908/09080401

[v] http://www.dentophobie.ch/english/dental-phobia-fear-dentist.html

[vi] https://www.softwareadvice.com/resources/how-patients-use-online-reviews/

[vii] http://www.dentistryiq.com/articles/2014/08/how-dental-patients-use-online-reviews.html

[viii] https://www.merriam-webster.com/dictionary/communication

[ix] Barnes (2015), https://patimes.org/damaging-effects-micromanagement/

[x] Wallen (2015), https://www.pluralsight.com/blog/business-professional/why-micromanagement-is-bad

[xi] Wilkins (2014), https://hbr.org/2014/11/signs-that-youre-a-micromanager

[xii] Saleh (2017). https://www.invespcro.com/blog/customer-acquisition-retention/

www.ingramcontent.com/pod-product-compliance
Lightning Source LLC
Chambersburg PA
CBHW050526190326
41458CB00045B/6717/J